ELASTIC

ENDORSEMENTS

Rebecca puts words to our uncertainties and vulnerabilities in thinking about our leadership. The thoughtfully gathered expressions and stories within her latest book encourage us to effort forward, together, with purpose and intent. *ELASTIC* compassionately invites you in to pause, reflect, and stretch—just enough.

Jodi Ball
Director, J Consulting Group, Canada

To stretch, under stress, and not snap is a path that so many leaders desire to walk but struggle to navigate. In this book, Rebecca's words help point the way in bright neon signs. Packed with equal parts aspiration and application, *ELASTIC* is a must read for leaders who want to learn the skills necessary to transform the way they lead and multiply their impact on the world around them.

Shane Hatton
Author of *Let's Talk Culture–The Conversations You Need to Create The Team You Want*, Australia

Rebecca has tied together a set of post-pandemic era skillsets that are the new essentials for leaders. Following her metaphor, *ELASTIC* inspires readers to explore their own personal opportunities to bend and flex, or where perhaps an anchor point needs to be adjusted. It also uncovers exciting areas for future research and development of leaders in an era of increasing disruption and change management. This book is a great read for emerging leaders, especially in the non-profit sector where often leaders are wearing many hats and struggling to stretch without snapping. Find your anchor point. Stretch with purpose. Know your boundaries.

Jennifer Juste
Municipal Transportation Planning Manager, Canada

Rebecca Sutherns has an easy straightforward way of sharing valuable information. Through her conversational writing she lays the framework in *ELASTIC* to help readers explore what it means to be intentionally and optimally stretchy. Rebecca's signature presence is "warm energy inviting connection, insight, and alignment."

Alicia King
Public Affairs Officer, Forest Service, U.S. Department of Agriculture, USA

Read this book! Unless you are happy swimming in the chronic and chaotic stress of your organization. Most organizations get to a place where they feel they are (constantly) about to snap. Overworked, overwhelming, or just over it! *ELASTIC* is the most elegant, practical, and perfectly fitting answer to this strain.

Chad Littlefield
Author, Speaker and Co-founder at We and Me, USA

I love this book—*ELASTIC* leadership sums up everything that is required from leaders in these weird and wonderful times.

Lisa O'Neill
Author, Speaker and CEO of Thought Leaders, New Zealand

Whether you are an experienced leader or just beginning your foray into unleashing human potential, this book is chock full of 'aha' moments and practical applications. Rebecca's ability to effortlessly integrate her practice, the theorists and her savvy observations are nothing short of miraculous. This book offers a glimpse into why Rebecca is considered among the best, whether leading groups in a church basement, executive board rooms or on the world stage. *ELASTIC* delivers just the 'stretch' you need to thrive in today's tumultuous ecosystem.

Katie Soles
Principal, Soles & Company Inc., Canada

An essential read for leaders. Rebecca is one of the most well-read people I know, and reading this book did not disappoint. You are taken on a journey of unravelling the core metaphor, acronym, and principles. Rebecca shares relatable stories to help navigate the world we are living in now. The concept of 'optimum elasticity' is brilliant, and I have already applied several of the practical steps to improve, amplify and build the 7 core qualities. The delightful added benefit of reading this book, is you get a fast track to learning the best bits from so many other books.

Ross Thornley
Author of *Moonshot Innovation* and *Decoding AQ*, United Kingdom

How can we maintain our energy in the midst of uncertainty? That might be the quintessential question of the past few years. Thankfully, Dr. Sutherns tackles that question with the ingenuity, compassion, and thoughtfulness that it needs. I hope you're ready to strengthen your stretch!

Dr. Dave Whiteside
Director of Insights, YMCA WorkWell, Canada

ELASTIC

STRETCH
WITHOUT SNAPPING
OR SNAPPING BACK

DR. REBECCA SUTHERNS, CPF

First published in 2023 by Hambone Publishing
Melbourne, Australia

Cover Design by Oliver Sutherns
Typesetting and Book Design by David W. Edelstein
Editing by Mish Phillips, Lexi Wight and Emily Stephenson
Case study assistance by Susan Fish

For information, contact:
Dr. Rebecca Sutherns
rebecca@rebeccasutherns.com
www.rebeccasutherns.com

ISBNs:
978-1-9995761-5-8 (paperback)
978-1-9995761-6-5 (ebook)
978-1-9995761-7-2 (audiobook)

To the first cohort of ELASTIC workshop participants. Thank you for your willingness to learn and experiment alongside me. Your insights have made this book better, and your encouragement got it done.

A mind, once stretched by a new idea,
never regains its original dimensions.
~Oliver Wendell Holmes

Contents

PART ONE

The Background

In spite of illness, in spite even of the arch-enemy, sorrow,
one can remain alive long past the usual date
of disintegration if one is unafraid of change,
insatiable in intellectual curiosity, interested in big things,
and happy in small ways.
~Edith Wharton

CONTEXT

Who doesn't want to "remain alive long past the usual date of disintegration"! Edith Wharton was the chosen subject of my Grade 13 English Independent Study, and I've enjoyed diving back into her work these many years later. I hope as you read her words here, you are feeling "insatiable in intellectual curiosity, interested in big things, and happy in small ways." But not many people I know are feeling "unafraid of change" right now. Currently three years into the COVID 19 pandemic, unpredictability has been revealed and amplified it, and many of us are weary. This book is intended to ease that weariness by equipping us to face uncertainty and volatility with a bit more courage and a dose of flexibility.

The backstory

Sometimes I spend too much time describing the context and providing the background—too long setting the stage. Yet here I go again. Why? Because I'm a fan of going slowly at the start to get results quickly at the end. It's a pattern I embrace in community engagement, in strategic planning, and in writing. It creates shared vocabulary and understanding which allow our collaborative momentum to build. You may have heard the proverb, "If you want to go fast, go alone. If you want to go far, go together." I believe that it is possible to go both fast and far together. Framing the context sets us up with the best opportunity to do this.

My context is shaped by my role as someone who has been facilitating collaborative planning for 25 years, mostly with large nonprofits, universities, health organizations, and local governments in Canada. Over that time, I have become more convinced that organizations need to read and understand their context in order to create a relevant road map for the future. I describe my approach to strategic planning in detail in *Sightline*[1], but let me highlight that I do not believe planning requires clairvoyance. Rather than positioning themselves as accurate predictors of the future, leaders need to be people who pay attention to signals and stay true to their organization's mission and goals as they adapt to an uncertain, unknowable future.

Responsiveness to context is key, yet in recent years, "pivot" has become an almost dirty word—certainly cause for eye-rolling. But we keep needing, seeing, and doing it nonetheless. The evolution of my course, Building Engagement in Digital Meetings, became symbolic of this increasing pace of change and the need to respond to it. Initially, the course was attractive to early adopters prepared to experiment with online delivery, then eventually to those reluctant participants who could no longer hunker down and wait for things to return to normal. Later, the course became populated by those whose online meetings had become stale and they were craving new tips and tricks for increasing digital connection one more time. All this happened within just a couple of years. Concurrently, I added a course called Tired Leaders Leading Tired Teams to my training repertoire, and it filled up even more quickly. My coaching clients described feeling depleted. People were being asked to stretch in too many directions at once, for too long. It all felt acutely unsustainable, yet there was no end in sight.

So, I began looking for sustainable ways to maintain energy in the midst of uncertainties that weren't going away. I read a lot, and started routinely asking other people what was working for them. I paid attention to the analogies that were resonating. And, gradually, ELASTIC emerged.

The times

A thorough analysis of the major socioeconomic trends facing our world is certainly beyond the scope of this book. But those trends do provide an important backdrop to the ideas we are about to explore. More than that, they speak to the relevance of being an ELASTIC leader. The climate crisis; political and religious polarization; global health emergencies; advances in technology such as digitization, artificial intelligence, and big data; more serious grappling with indigenous reconciliation, racism, and other forms of oppression and exclusion; workforce transformations; massive demographic shifts... it is a dizzying and uncertain yet exciting time to be alive.

The pace of change is accelerating. Humans are not adapting as quickly as technology is changing. We know this, empirically and viscerally. You hardly need me to tell you that we continually need to stretch, and to safeguard our well-being in the process.

As the world of work is changing, employers report a higher emphasis on skills building versus contracting, hiring, redeploying, or releasing staff.[2] And these skills are not just technical in nature. Continually adapting to new ways of working is frequently identified as a foundational skill, alongside "softer and more advanced cognitive skills" such as leadership, critical thinking, and empathy.[3,4] "Being ready, willing, and able to adapt faster to just about anything is perhaps the most critical skill we all need now."[5] Our ability to cope with uncertainty and to adapt are consistently among the highest predictors of future employability.

As David Rock notes in his assessment of future leadership trends, "In the absence of certainty, clarity can be a soothing balm."[6] It is my hope that this book will provide some much-needed relief by clearly describing what is happening, what is working, and what might help.

The purpose

Reading this book will help you develop a clearer picture and deeper understanding of purposeful, adaptive leadership. You'll learn strategies to build it in yourself and others, in ways that are both productive and sustainable. You'll also be inspired by examples of how community-minded leaders are putting these principles into practice. Whether you're a seasoned leader or just starting out, feeling over-stretched or under-challenged, I trust this book will provide you with reassurance, wise counsel, and encouragement as you seek your optimal level of stretch: the right amount, neither too far nor for too long.

Within this purpose, I have three objectives in writing this book. The first is descriptive. The book's central metaphor provides shared vocabulary for something we've all experienced in the recent past. A shared language is not only expressive, it is also validating. Labelling our experience, even provisionally, can help us make sense of it. It strengthens a sense of belonging and being seen and offers a powerful resource for moving forward productively together. Have you ever spent time in a place where people spoke a different language than you, and experienced the frustration that comes from communication being limited, slow, and stilted? If so, I don't need to say more.

My second aim is practical. I hope to strengthen people's ability to live and lead intentionally in the face of uncertainty and change. More specifically, my invitation is for you to stretch productively without overdoing it. All of us need to learn this, but my main audience is people who are attentive to their own behaviour and in a position to influence the behaviour of others. I call these people "leaders" throughout the book, but I'd invite you to hear the inclusive intent behind that term. You don't have to be a formal leader for this book to be relevant to you. We all need to challenge ourselves—but not too much—and to be deliberate about the shape we want our lives to take. Even if you don't consider yourself a leader within an organizational hierarchy, if you want to make choices that help you and others thrive, you're a leader in my books (but as a side note, why do you not see yourself as a leader? Perhaps that is the subject of another book...).

My third objective is inspirational. I intend to showcase the fine work of Canadian community sector leaders, honouring their commitment and skill as I mark my 25th year in business. One element of my practice is to run a monthly book club that curates and summarizes recent titles to help busy leaders stay current when they don't read as much as they'd like to. (Did you know that by some estimates the average American reads two or three books per year, while CEOs read four to five books per month?).[7] Frankly, I'm tired of every leadership book highlighting the experience of the same very few, very large corporations, most often in Silicon Valley, as if their experience is easily applicable to the rest of us. There is much to be learned from mission-driven, modestly sized, community-minded organizations. They are not all running on a shoestring out of a church basement. Many are sophisticated, highly impactful, well-led operations. Their contributions not just to our economy and our social fabric, but to our leadership learning, deserve to be recognized.

THE STRUCTURE

Within those three objectives, this book is structured to explain the same idea in three different styles. You can read all three sections together, or choose the approach that aligns best with your learning preferences. Combining all three lenses will undoubtedly give you the richest appreciation of its message, but each section has value on its own. Choose your own adventure!

The power of a metaphor

The opening section treats ELASTIC as an extended metaphor for responsive, intentional leadership that challenges us toward optimal performance without doing damage. I encourage you to find your ZOnE—your Zone of Optimal Elasticity.

A good metaphor can bring an idea to life. It's a vivid analogy that helps make a comparison more visual, powerful, persuasive, and memorable. It's an anchor for memorization, and it can also deepen understanding and insight, sometimes helping us get unstuck.[8,9] But metaphors are useful until they are not. They are not exact. They can easily be forced or overdone. The metaphor needs to serve the learning, not the other way around. That's why at times I will highlight the limitations of the metaphor of elasticity, acknowledging when the analogy ceases to be helpful.

Used judiciously, metaphors can be a terrific learning tool... until they get stretched too far.

I had been playing with the metaphor of elasticity in leadership, courtesy of a workshop I'd repeatedly led on thriving during the pandemic. I could see some organizations had become a bit nutty, repeatedly overshooting the mark or manically changing direction too often, while exhausting their people as a result. At the same time, others were stuck in nostalgia, waiting for things to "go back to normal" and thereby missing opportunities to stay relevant. The organizations catching my attention were finding a zone of appropriate stretch—not none, but not too far. Known in some contexts as "The Goldilocks Zone," living in that "nailing it" space seemed to represent an optimum zone for thriving in this prolonged season of widespread uncertainty.

The cheesiness of an acronym

The second section unpacks an acronym of the word ELASTIC that highlights seven promising leadership practices to support the optimal performance suggested by the metaphor.

An acronym is a learning aid that makes concepts easier to remember. Acronyms are mnemonics, devices used to ease the pressure on our overburdened memory. They are a proven instructional method that work best when they also paint a vivid picture linked the concept they describe. Think of them as an external hard drive for your short-term memory, a temporary extra storage space for information you will need to draw on later. Brief mnemonics are better than long ones, as our short-term memory most effectively stores seven items (phew!) plus or minus two.[10,11,12]

The elements of the ELASTIC acronym were developed to capture characteristics in leaders I admire, that I feel are underrepresented or poorly explained in current business literature. Energy, Likeability,

Adaptability, Strategy, Trust, Imagination and Curiosity. They are not exhaustive, but they are easy to remember!

Here's how it happened: I was sitting on the dock at our new-to-us cottage, on vacation in 2021. I started making a list of concepts I was curious to explore in my practice over the coming year. It started with "collective imagination" and built from there. Curiosity came next, then energy.

As my daydreaming evolved, I found myself playing with five concepts, and rearranging the letters EASIC into whatever word I could come up with. Having spent much of the pandemic playing Wordle—an online daily word game that involves rearranging letters to make a five-letter word—this was a familiar task to me! Nothing came to mind, and when I looked it up, "SAICE" was the only word containing those five letters. It was listed as having "no associated definition." Not very helpful.

Eventually, likeability and trust emerged through more research, and ELASTIC was born.

I wish I were in a position to say that these seven qualities, and only these, contribute empirically to a robust demonstration of human elasticity, but we're not there yet. This is an exploratory book. It's structured to help us make sense of what we've experienced and to remember some ways we might want to behave more often.

The inspiration of examples

Finally, the third section offers case studies that leverage story to give you a window into real and recent experiences where organizations have demonstrated these ELASTIC qualities.

We all need to trust that when the rubber meets the road, the ideas we've been test-driving will deliver. Case studies offer recent, accessible examples of people who are using ELASTIC skills in real life. Their experiences inspire us to apply the principles we've learned in creative ways we may not otherwise have considered. These examples show as much as they tell.

Storytelling expert Lisa Gerber of Big Leap Creative highlights showing rather than telling as a way to build credibility.[13] It's one of three superpowers of stories, alongside breathing life into facts and statistics as a pathway to empathy and action; and helping us make meaning out of complexity. Jason Thompson of Storyist concurs:

> *"The most wonderous power of great storytelling is the ability to connect with people on an emotional level. When we share something that makes others feel something deeply, we create an opportunity to inspire action and drive change. Stories that are well told enhance attention, create anticipation and increase retention. It is our greatest tool in making meaningful connections with a diverse set of audiences."*[14]

One of the mantras of Thought Leaders Business School—in which I serve as a faculty member—is, "Be inspired by the company you keep." These case studies provide you with inspiring company. These are real people I admire, working in real organizations committed to building community and equity in ways that inspire me. Examples such as these help us see what is possible. They encourage us to consider how we could adapt their approaches to make sense in our worlds.

The richness of co-creation

I've become curious about disrupting my traditional understanding of what being an author requires. When I think of someone writing a book, I think of them sitting alone at a desk for hours, perhaps working on a typewriter. Archaic perhaps, but our mental models and biases deeply inform our practice. Although writing a book can appear to be a solitary activity (and much of the time it is), every acknowledgements section will tell you that authors rarely work alone. A team is required to get a book out into the world. For this book, I wanted to explore a different way of creating it. I decided to build it collaboratively from the outset, explicitly. I invited others to join me on the journey. An insightful, willing group of guinea pigs gathered monthly in 2021/2022 to explore these concepts of ELASTIC leadership aloud in real time with me. Rather than waiting until my acknowledgements section to thank them, I'd like to honour them here: Sandra Allison, Sandra Austin, Jodi Ball, Glenna Banda, Stuart Beumer, Meredith Burpee, Adrienne Crowder, Kim Cusimano, Amanda Etches, Meeta Gandhi, Christine Hyde, Jennifer Juste, Ron Kadyschuk, Linda Kenny, Alicia King, Karen Martin Schiedel, Anne McArthur, Marcia Scheffler, Katie Soles, Emily Stahl, Tim Sutherns, and Mark Valcic. Their openness to trying something new together was encouraging, and their insights were too numerous to footnote properly throughout. In many ways, their names should appear as co-authors. I am grateful for their support.

Similarly, the experience of gathering the case studies conversationally and co-writing them with long-time friend Susan Fish is another example of how writing has become social.

This experience of explicit co-creation not only contributed content and refined the ideas in this book, it also continually reminded me that every book represents a work in progress. We are constantly revising our thinking, and a book is simply a snapshot in time of how far we've come on our learning journey. Meeting with this group allowed me to hold my thinking loosely. It also showed me the truth of my mantra: "Multiple perspectives are protective." None of us knows the full picture, and collaboration reduces blind spots. I wonder what else we traditionally think of as an individual activity that could benefit from happening collectively?

PART TWO

The Metaphor

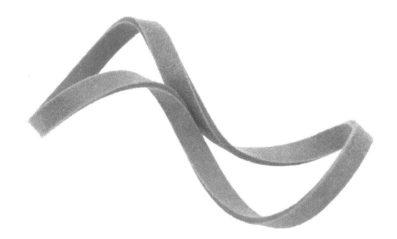

Before you read any further, grab something stretchy, like a rubber band. Give it a tug. What do you notice about it?

In this section, I'll dive into an extended metaphor that compares an elastic to human behaviour as we respond to external pressures. When you consider how you are currently doing, perhaps in your paid work or broader life, how stretched are you feeling? Where might you fit on the diagram below?

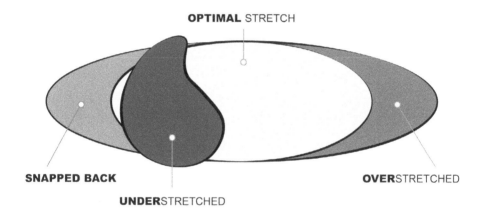

OPTIMAL STRETCH

SNAPPED BACK

UNDERSTRETCHED

OVERSTRETCHED

ELASTICS

...are, um... elastic.

As extension, so force.
~Robert Hooke, 1676
(Often translated to "Stress is proportional to strain.")

am no physicist. But I do know that elasticity is a physical property that allows a material to stretch when subjected to an external force and then rebound to its previous state. Elastic theory is useful in predicting how things will respond to loads. Elastic materials don't only stretch, they also compress and then return to their original shape from that coiled position. They store potential energy and then release it when the external force is removed (think of a diving board). Interestingly, in science this quality is also known as resilience.[15] Elastic materials perform at their best when optimally stretched. It's a quality that is relatively rare.

Can you see already how this metaphor of elasticity can apply to people under stress? In recent years, external events have stretched, squeezed, and distorted us. We've resisted, been deformed, stored potential energy that temporarily had nowhere to be released. Then we returned, to varying degrees, to our original shape—or at least were expected to do so.

Most materials get thinner and longer when stretched—like dough being rolled out. People too tend to feel tighter when we're stretched. The same can be true in reverse: we are more relaxed and flexible with people who energize rather than stress us, aren't we? But a few materials, known as auxetics, actually do the opposite of what we are used to; some polymers, for example, expand in the transverse direction when stretched—stretching causes their crumples to unfold.[16]

Sit with that for a moment. Imagine if we became auxetic people, such that being stretched didn't make us more tense, but rather caused our crumples to unfold!

In economic theory, elasticity refers to how far one element stretches when it is influenced by another. The key point is that we cannot know the elasticity of something until it is affected by an external force. Any of us who have risen to the challenge of a crisis and thought, "I didn't know I had it in me," will feel the resonance of this element of the metaphor.

Have you ever needed an elastic band and not been able to find one? If so, then you know how handy elastics are and how problematic it is not to have one (think ponytail). Consider how valuable it is that our skin and muscles demonstrate elasticity—if it didn't, those of us who have borne children would look even droopier than we already do! Elasticity is a useful property. Imagine its absence—we couldn't stretch at all without breaking, or if we could temporarily, we may not be able to find our way back to any semblance of normal.

You also know how adaptable elastics are; useful in multiple contexts. Consider how the same rubber band could work to hold pencils, stalks of broccoli, or a stack of important envelopes together. They can also handle jobs that appear outsized, holding things together much bigger than themselves.

Yet elastics are not infinitely interchangeable. They come in different strengths and sizes and have different capacities. You clearly wouldn't use a tiny orthodontic elastic (designed to gradually straighten your teeth) for bungee jumping. People also have different best-use cases, don't we!

Elastics are flexible, but within limits. They always have some give, but not an infinite amount. Not only could they snap if overstretched (more on that later), they also don't work if they are too loose. Their usefulness depends on being under some pressure to perform. Flexibility in elastic materials is not infinite; it must always be counterbalanced with strength.

To varying degrees, elastic materials resist being stretched. It is why resistance bands are effective at the gym. The resistance band elastics are themselves the external force, testing and strengthening the elasticity of our muscles. And you and I both know our muscles resist the task! As the resistance gets more forceful, we get stronger.

And therein lies the magic. We are all subject to strains, but some of us grow through them. As former CEO of Intel, Andy Grove is known to have said, "Bad companies are destroyed by crisis. Good companies survive them. Great companies are improved by them."[17]

I trust you can hear several ways these elastic qualities speak to your situation. As I highlight some of the potential applications of this metaphor, understand that I do so in pencil, not permanent marker! You can make your own connections. But below are a few to get you started.

- While the impacts of COVID 19 are not equally distributed, they are uniformly deep, widespread, and lasting. The pressures of pandemic life have been repeatedly removed and reapplied over time. As a result, all of us have been required to stretch and rebound repeatedly and in multiple ways, and we are only just beginning to sort out the implications of that experience, personally and collectively.

- Elasticity is an asset when it helps us bounce back from stress. Without it, we would be brittle and break. Yet our shape cannot help but be different as a result of what we have experienced. Rebounding to our original form may no longer be possible or desirable. I notice this pressure specifically in terms of return-to-the-office conversations, where employees are resisting the expectation that they will resume previous work arrangements as if nothing has changed in the meantime.

- Unlike in materials science, people have a choice about the shape they will assume after being stretched, rather than automatically returning to an old one. Let's be explicit and intentional in making that choice where we can be. And to the extent that leaders' decisions constrain that choice, let's not be oblivious to the lasting effects of the traumas people have experienced when we ask them to resume old duties in old ways.

- In human lives, it is my sincere hope that flexibility and strength are not inversely proportional to each other. We should not have to choose between them. But the relative proportions of their coexistence do warrant further exploration in context.

- What might it take for us to get bigger not smaller when we are stretched or compressed by external pressures? "Be more auxetic" isn't exactly catchy as a hashtag or on a T-shirt, but it is what's needed. What a dramatic mindset shift to think of being stretched as "unfolding our crumples!"

Let's dig deeper.

...are stretchy.

The soft and supple will prevail.
~Lao Tzu

An unstretchable elastic is useless. Think of an elastic waistband that's too big, or a broken guitar string. Better yet, grab a rubber band from your kitchen drawer and see what you can do with it without stretching it. Not much. It doesn't perform the purpose for which it's intended, and the benefits of its stretchiness are wasted. Stretching is good.

To stretch, an elastic requires a directly proportional outside force. It does not stretch of its own accord. Stress stretches it, and that is not a bad thing. The stress allows the elastic to demonstrate its capabilities that would otherwise be invisible or go unused. Stretching also allows an elastic to stay supple. I recently picked up a rubber band that had sat on my desk while I was away all summer. Even a gentle stretch resulted in it snapping in my hand. It had become brittle from underuse.

In his book *Stretch*,[18] Scott Sonenshein explores the benefits of stretching for people, describing it as an opportunity to make the most of existing resources rather than constantly needing to acquire new ones. He writes of the positive ways in which constraints make us more resourceful and how assuming an attitude of psychological ownership over our challenging experiences actually makes us more expansive. For Sonenshein, stretching is the opposite of chasing. Even in a context of abundant resources, he highly recommends it.

Stretching is always necessary to demonstrate elasticity, but in people it is experienced differently when it is voluntary versus involuntary. There is a different positive energy that comes from testing our limits in ways that are chosen, for example by stretching our imagination or taking on an ambitious challenge such as climbing Mount Kilimanjaro, compared to involuntarily being stretched to our limits through unchosen hardship. In his celebrated book *Flow*,[19] Mihaly Csikszentmihalyi writes that our best moments are not passive, receptive ones, but usually occur when we are voluntarily stretched to our limits, accomplishing something both difficult and worthwhile. We have a visceral understanding of how stretching is experienced differently depending on the amount of agency and choice we bring to it.

Consider the familiar business practice of setting stretch goals. These goals are deliberately challenging and ambitious. They require high effort and high risk, with the intention of inspiring growth and commitment and countering complacency. They set targets above normal standards to attract exponential rewards. But they can also create frustration if forced upon those implementing them. Ironically, research demonstrates that those who need them are least likely to achieve them, and in the absence of a clear pathway to get to them, the ambitiousness of stretch goals can be experienced as unrealistic and frustrating.[20, 21]

In *Collaborating with the Enemy*,[22] Adam Kahane describes stretch collaboration as being a state in which we give up fantasies of harmony, certainty, and compliance and instead embrace the messy realities of co-creation, experimentation, and even discord. This is an excellent example of stretch that is both voluntary and painful, which seems to be the way of it much of the time.

It may also be true that stretching is painful not because it is pulling you into new, unwelcome areas but because it is holding you back from fulfilling your potential. Consider the string of an archer's bow when it is pulled tightly backwards. It is stretched taut and can only propel an arrow forward when the force is removed. The greater the stretch, the more the tension builds, and the farther the arrow will travel upon release. Elasticity is required to generate eventual forward momentum, but the stretch itself can hold you back. It is useful to consider whether a stretching situation is propelling you forward into new, uncomfortable territory, or is in fact holding you back from going there.

An elastic also requires a fixed point or an anchor from which it can stretch. In the absence of that anchor, it floats rather than stretches. This characteristic is so obvious to us, we rarely notice it, yet once it is drawn to our attention, we can't unsee it. One part of the elastic must stay still to permit the rest of it to stretch. Consider how Spiderman gets around—he anchors his web to one building before sending a stretchy line out to the next one.

Applied to people (not just superheroes!), this metaphor of

stretchiness requires us to discern what is fixed and what is flexible in our own lives. Where will we stay tethered, and in what other directions might that allow us to stretch? We often resist being constrained, thrashing like a toddler buckled unwillingly into her car seat. But in the context of elasticity, restricting movement in at least one area unleashes potential in others.

The challenge here lies not just in having a fixed point, but in making sure our anchor is well-chosen. It can, for example, be a negative reference point or a limiting belief that is holding us back in unhealthy ways. How much better to be grounded instead in foundational values that provide rock-solid security, or a north star around which all other things orbit and can find their safe place!

The corollary is to make sure that we are not shifting and adapting indiscriminately in areas of our lives that would be better off staying fixed. Being stretchy or adaptable may not be what is most needed, in context. The combination of flexibility and strength is particularly important here, as strength of conviction needs to complement responsiveness when decisions about when and how far to adapt must be made. This reminds me of clients who were so committed to pivoting that they didn't stick with one course of action long enough to discern if it was actually working well. Experimentation is great, but it doesn't serve its purpose if we move on to a new experiment before the results are in.

Particularly over these past few years, you may have found your "fixed points" needing to shift. It can feel deeply unsettling when elements we thought wouldn't or couldn't change start to wobble, especially when it happens across multiple domains at once. No one would have expected the global travel industry, the education system, the sites of our work, and the way we access health care to have fundamentally changed all at the same time, for instance! It is possible and often necessary for our anchor points to move over time, but our ability to stretch depends on having at least one fixed point at a time.

Stretching is most effective when it happens gradually. Kinesiologists would concur when it comes to the effective stretching of human muscles. Sudden stretching increases the risk of injury. Learning to be more flexible rarely happens at sprint pace. In behavioural science, Julia Galef invites us to let new evidence stretch our theory of how things work, until that theory can no longer hold. She encourages us to get curious about it without panicking, as the process is rarely sudden.[23]

In *The Power of Moments*, Chip and Dan Heath describe the benefits of being pushed by a mentor. That push leads to a stretch, which creates a memorable moment of self-insight. Pushing is counterintuitive though, as our instinct is to protect people we care about from risk. They go on to say, "The promise of stretching is not success, it's learning, [...] it's the promise of gleaning answers to some of the most important and vexing questions of our lives: what do we want? What can we do? Who can we be? What can we endure? [...] We will never know our reach unless we stretch."[24]

...can snap.

Only those who will risk going too far can possibly
find out how far one can go.
~TS Eliot

But sometimes stretching is neither voluntary nor gradual.

Materials have an "elastic limit." That's the threshold where elastic behaviour becomes plastic behaviour. Rubber bands, neglected or stretched too far too fast, can become brittle and break. Where that limit is depends on the nature of the material itself.

To what extent is the same true in humans? Do we too have limits to our tensile strength?

We assume we do.

Have you ever attended a yoga class and heard someone say, "I'm just not flexible"? Similarly, it's not uncommon to hear some variation of, "We cannot stretch too far in too many directions at once." We perceive elasticity to be a zero-sum game, with a fixed amount of flexibility to go around. However, in the realm of human behaviour, people can learn to become stretchier.

Unlike physical materials that have a fixed amount of flexibility, recent research suggests that the components that contribute to human adaptability can be improved over time. Neuroscience is teaching us that these attributes are malleable and can be learned. We can learn our way into improving our elasticity. Dimensions of adaptability such as grit, resilience, mental flexibility, and team support are socially constructed and therefore changeable. Interestingly, maintaining a growth mindset is also a component of adaptability. Assuming our adaptability is a fixed quantity is the opposite of that.

Our behavioural stretch tolerance is improved through a combination of stretching and strength training over time. Stretching alone does not make us stronger. Strength training involves repetition of known and increasingly challenging moves, with recovery time in between. Without strength, we risk losing stability when we stretch and need outside help to support us. In recent years, those outside supports that might have come through relationships were strained, due to isolation and the exhaustion of everyone being stretched at the same time.

Physiologically, our ability to stretch our muscles is less about muscle length or tautness and more about what our nervous system considers safe to do. Our stretch reflex is a defence mechanism to prevent injury from stretching too far. Flexibility is therefore a communication issue that involves reassuring our nervous system that a particular range of motion is safe to move into.[25, 26] The applications into human behaviour are multiple here. How often have we resisted a new adventure not because we were physically incapable of its demands, but because our brain was confusing unfamiliar with unsafe?

I have three daughters who were all competitive dancers. They were the only members of their dance team to be unable to do the splits, despite years of concerted effort and training. We chalked it up to genetics, with my apologies. When their younger brother wanted to improve his hamstring flexibility for volleyball, he researched different approaches and went from only being able to reach his knees when folded forward to putting his hands fully and easily on the ground. He did not repeat the same moves and expect different results than they had seen; he changed his strategy. He used weights, leveraging his strength to increase his flexibility. And while training techniques matter, so too does the belief that improvement is possible. We will not go after something we believe is impossible to attain.

Overstretching does remain a risk, however. After a workout, you can feel extra warm and it's easy to push yourself too far, as your muscles in that state are limber. They are also quite tired. Does this sound familiar, particularly post-pandemic? I can think of numerous examples of coaching clients who reported taking on extra responsibilities, thinking they could handle them (or didn't have a choice not to), and those added tasks wound up being their final step on the path toward burnout. Jim Moss of YMCA WorkWell describes burnout as a process that imperceptibly gains momentum as it worsens. We think we have remaining capacity, or time to course correct, yet what we perceived as remaining runway is actually a cliff.[27]

If our capacity to stretch does in fact reach breaking point, can we only know once it's too late? Can we only identify 'too far' once we've gone past it, or are we able to recognize the signs preventatively before we've hit that point? Our stretchiness may exhibit what James Clear refers to as a Goldilocks Rule: our peak motivation sits at the edge of our current abilities, where a task is not too easy and not too hard.[28] That's the Zone of Optimal Elasticity. Can we pull back before we reach the edge?

In our muscles, a good way to prevent hyperextension is to maintain a small bend in the joints instead of locking them.[29] I am reminded of the benefits of maintaining a ready stance in tennis, with slightly bent knees, bouncing gently on the balls of the feet, ready to accept whatever shot comes our way. We are much more likely to move nimbly and return the shot effectively, contrasted with a low success rate if the volley finds us frozen with locked knees and a mind fixed on receiving a deep forehand. What might the equivalent "ready stance" be in leadership? I suspect it has to do with maintaining what I call "responsive capacity"—margins or a buffer zone that allow us space to respond to unexpected events. When developing organizational strategy, I recommend building in this capacity both individually and collectively, as a calendar or a workforce filled right to its edges has little room to cope with unpredictability. And greeting the unexpected is a surprisingly predictable occurrence!

Thankfully, our ability to create buffers and readiness does not have to happen alone. Human adaptability is both an individual and a team pursuit. If we extend the elasticity metaphor to include many rubber bands attached together end to end, into what we used to call a "jumpsie rope" on my elementary school playground, we can visualize the expanded stretch that comes from collective action and support. By reframing a task as requiring a collaborative effort, each member of the chain is not pulled to full capacity, yet the cumulative stretchiness of the whole chain is considerably increased by sharing the load. Many hands do indeed make light work, even when it comes to stretching. Snapping a jumpsie rope is close to impossible. (We tried it once and got in trouble for leaving the playground in an effort to stretch it past its breaking point!)

...can snap back.

Remember that returning to its original shape is part of the definition of a material's elasticity. Rebounding is in its DNA. There is no external force required to bring the material back to that form; it automatically reverts to what it knew before. That's its default setting, with no additional instructions required.

This is an element of elasticity that easily translates to human behaviour. We tend to revert to what we know and to what is comfortable, particularly when we are under stress or when stress has been relieved at last.

Default settings are selected automatically unless a viable alternative is specified. They are handy, as they help us save time and effort.[30] Daniel Kahneman's research refers to this as 'fast thinking' that occurs with relative cognitive ease.[31] Imagine if we had to make a conscious decision every time we needed to take an action. Should I bite this apple? Should I pick up this pen? Is it a good idea to put my feet on the floor to get out of bed? This level of conscious decision making would be utterly exhausting.

As the stress of the pandemic has [intermittently] subsided, people have found themselves reverting to their defaults—relatively automatically returning to what they did before, often more quickly than they thought they might, for better or worse.

As with stretching, the pace at which one returns to an original shape matters in the material world. Some of the strongest known natural materials, such as spider webs and even the filaments in mussels, possess not only tensile strength, but also an ability to relax slowly.[32] Humans can learn from nature here: perhaps returning to a previous shape slowly increases the likelihood that we will pause and consciously decide if we are following a route we intend to take.

Default settings save time and mental energy, but they also make things invisible to us—like the piles of clutter in our homes that we only notice when guests are coming over. As Dr. Jason Fox suggests in *How to Lead a Quest*, speed and efficiency come at the expense of accuracy, empathy, and relevance.[33] Which is why it may surprise us when we find that although we have rebounded, our new shape no longer fits our old behaviour patterns. When we pause to notice, we realize that not only did the context change, but we have changed too.

Massive transformations in work arrangements are the clearest current example of this. Many corporate return-to-the office policies and processes have failed miserably for this very reason, and it is frequently the leaders who are surprised by this reaction. They assumed that people would simply return to the office and resume business as usual. As one CEO said to me, "I never would have thought I had to convince workers to come into work!" Yet many of those same workers have been changed by the experience of the pandemic. They have experienced what it is like to work from home and have found they enjoy it. They are more productive. They commute less. They have more discretionary time and report better work-life balance. For some, this historical turning point has led to a fundamental reset in perspective, leading them to pursue alternative career options altogether. In a recent study of 70,000 federal public service workers in Canada, just 10% were interested in returning to the office full time, with 60% preferring a work-from-home scenario.[34] An expectation of unquestioningly returning to old ways of working can make leaders seem oblivious or tone deaf—even if they are acting within their legal or traditional rights.

In *Competing in the New World of Work*, Keith Ferrazzi and his co-authors encourage a more thoughtful return:

> *"What if this new world of work ended up permanently tarred*
> *by its association with the pandemic? What if tradition and*
> *inertia proved to be so strong that all the bad old habits*
> *snapped back into effect as soon as the pandemic ended?*
> *Crises are so exhausting that it's natural to want to return*
> *to the comfort of the familiar. But if we were to do that and*
> *resume working the way we had before, such a return would*

be yet another disaster, one that would last long after the
pandemic had passed into history."[35]

Todd Henry, in his book *Die Empty*, described one chapter of his life this way, "Like a rubber band stretched beyond its elasticity, I simply couldn't return to normal."[36] I am confident many of us could say the same. When a rubber band has been extended around the same large item for too long, it loses its spring. It is no longer useful for its original purpose. It can neither stretch nor recover its old shape. We too have been invisibly but structurally changed by having been stretched too far for too long. There may be no going back.

When there is no going back

So where does this leave us?

It may leave us in the hallway.

My friend and colleague Nancy Watt introduced me to the term "The hell of the hallway." It happens when one door has closed and another one has yet to open. We can find ourselves in a holding pattern, waiting for the next opportunity.

These moments between departure and arrival are called liminal spaces. They are the transitional territory between states or seasons, and they are both necessary and uncomfortable. Liminal spaces are thresholds offering opportunities for reflection, growth, and creativity but also feelings of stress and unsettledness in the waiting for new possibilities to emerge.

It could be that before the next door opens, we need to embrace our new shape. Or to stretch even further, to find our new shape. We can't (or don't want to) return to old patterns, yet we aren't fit for our new ones quite yet.

James Clear writes that changing habits both requires and is a pathway to a change in belief. "Every action you take is a vote for the type of person you wish to become."[37] He suggests that new identities require new evidence. Our habits prove who we are becoming and can change our beliefs about ourselves.

Moving through a liminal space can't be rushed. In the midst, consider strategies such as journalling, conscious personal development through reading or podcasts, connecting with trusted friends, and/or hiring trained professionals such as a coach or therapist to help you reflect on and reframe your situation. Hold the process lightly—seasons of transition are disorienting, but they can be exciting and restorative too.[38]

GETTING IN
THE ZOnE

Consider where you marked yourself on this diagram. Your response might be different for various domains of your life (e.g., overall, at work, at home etc.) and at various times:

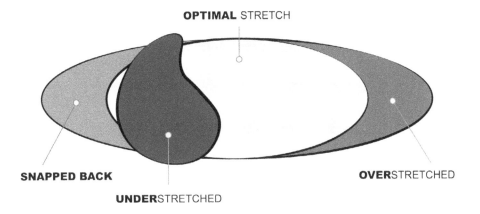

OPTIMAL STRETCH

SNAPPED BACK

UNDERSTRETCHED

OVERSTRETCHED

The goal is to head toward the middle or the Zone of Optimal Elasticity (the ZOnE). It's there you will most likely feel a sense of power and potential for impact, combined with a hint of nervous anticipation. You're challenged, but you have a bit of battery life left too. Congratulations! Go make the difference you were born to make.

If you find yourself languishing in the darker area, you may not be stretching enough to be challenged or impactful. Consider what you need to ramp up your mojo. Deep rest? A compelling goal? A change of scenery? New responsibilities? Someone to join you on the journey? Or it may be that you've lost your anchor and you can't stretch because you have come untethered. What are your fixed points that need to be identified or recommitted to, that will allow you to stretch from there?

If you are well left of centre, you might be snapping back unconsciously into old ways that do not fit or serve you any longer. The goal here is to be conscious and intentional in your decision making. Turn on your radar and pay attention. You may need to actively unlearn beliefs and habits that used to be helpful but are not anymore.[39] Perhaps you need to enlist the help of a coach. Are there brave conversations you've been putting off? Decisions you are hesitating to make but that won't leave your mind?

If you are right of centre, you are likely feeling overstretched, perhaps even on the brink of burnout. You've been stretched too far, too fast, for too long. What might it take to relieve some pressure? My favourite resources on addressing burnout are *Burnout: The Secret to Unlocking the Stress Cycle* by Emily and Amelia Nagoski[40] and *The Burnout Epidemic* by Jennifer Moss.[41] At the risk of sounding cliché, sleep, healthy nutrition, and exercise are likely a potent prescription for you. Are there choices in front of you that haven't felt like viable options for a while? Tap into your cognitive flexibility and remember there are more ways to solve this problem than you might be considering right now.

We can move in and out of these postures surprisingly often and quickly. A habit of checking our stretch is well worth developing, so we can find our way back to the ZOnE.

PART THREE

The Acronym

STRENGTHENING YOUR STRETCH

Like looking through a prism at a different angle, we will now turn our attention from the metaphor of elasticity to an acronym of ELASTIC. Each letter represents a different skill or currency leveraged by ELASTIC leaders: energy, likeability, adaptability, strategy, trust, imagination, and curiosity

Why these seven?

The seven qualities in the ELASTIC acronym are not the only ones that contribute to our stretchiness. But I am convinced they help. All of the qualities emerged as skills I've noticed in the leaders I most enjoy and admire. These qualities seem underrepresented, poorly explained, or unsubstantiated in current leadership writing. They are too often framed as fixed characteristics than learnable skills. They also make for interesting conversation. Although their initial selection was somewhat arbitrary on my part, born out of meandering exploration, you too will find them compelling enough to read on. This is a conversational book as much as an empirical one—an invitation to join a learning journey unfolding in [almost] real time.

Mutual reinforcement

Although I will address each of the seven elements separately for ease of recall and explanation, they should not be seen as independent silos. As you will notice in the descriptions that follow, they represent a complex, mutually reinforcing web. They can be inputs and/or outcomes for one another, often in unexpected ways. When I tried to map their interconnections, the resulting graphic looked like a plate of spaghetti!

For each letter, I'll draw on experience, research evidence, and imagination to consider what the skill or currency means, why it helps in our journey toward more ELASTIC leadership, and how to amplify it in real life.

ENERGY

The world belongs to the energetic
~Ralph Waldo Emerson

What it is and why we need it

I frequently begin facilitated digital meetings by inviting participants to type one word in the Chat describing their current state. I am amazed how often the word "weary" has appeared in recent months. People are tired. As one Canadian study found just five months into the pandemic, the number of working adults reporting unhealthy well-being scores had more than doubled since "the before times," and that number has stayed consistent since.

> "Employees are depleted, [...] relentless uncertainty in the workplace, along with a never-ending stream of social, economic, and financial pressures are draining. Many employees in our communities are understandably struggling to keep afloat—and it is burning them out."[42]

Against this backdrop of depletion, I believe that energy has become one of the most precious and important currencies we have, perhaps more valuable than money and time in some cases. Our energy is scarce, and we need to find more sustainable sources of it.

In identifying energy as a key trait of effective leaders, I do not mean to imply that all leaders must be highly extroverted and wildly enthusiastic. People do not need to be outgoing in a cheerleader-at-a-pep-rally way to exhibit a contagious, compelling energy. There is a steady energy that calms and depressurizes, alongside that which pumps us up.[43] Leaders' energy does not have to show up as inauthentic either (what Kate Bowler and others describes as toxic positivity).[44] I hope each of us has been in the presence of someone whose energy, quiet or loud, makes people around them better. Effective leaders model positive energy, and their energy sets the tone.

The energy of leaders drives culture. But energy is not neutral. Not all energy is positive energy. There is both a quantitative and a qualitative dimension to the energy leadership I'm referring to here, and my assumption is that effective leaders exhibit and offer energy of the positive kind.

"Positive energy" can sound a bit too vague; it's been called "an impossibly squishy subject."[45] Yet Deborah Martin's research demonstrates that positive energy is observable in the demeanour of colleagues. These energizers provide clear direction, as well as emotional and tactical support. They engage and communicate with others. They demonstrate enough competence to inspire others to work hard and develop their own competence, and they are genuine. Positive energy is not an aimless or static state. Instead, it is better understood as a social motivational force with direction and momentum.[46]

Positive energizers are significantly higher performers. People exposed to positive energizers in the workplace have higher personal well-being, job satisfaction, and engagement. Organizations with high energy have stronger cohesion, more orientation toward learning, and more creativity.[47]

Energy is both our fuel and our fuel gauge. High-energy leaders steward their energy well. This means not only being aware of their own energy but being aware of the effects their energy has on others. It can be contagious in a good way.[48] Energy management and monitoring is a leader's responsibility. Leaders should recognize what energizes and depletes people's energy, and serve as charging stations when they can. Leaders who understand their responsibility both to monitor and increase the energy of their colleagues and of their organization are leaders I want to follow.

We don't often think of energy as being an organizational trait; it is much more often used in reference to individuals. Occasionally, we notice the energy of teams, certainly in sports but also in communities banding together to address a crisis. But is it possible that organizations can be described as having energy? If so, where does that energy reside?

I am in the 25th year of my business and work with more than 50 organizations per year. I have witnessed organizations with energy, and those without. While they do tend to take on the personalities of those who lead and work in them, there are collective traits that seem to transcend individual styles and moods. That energy comes from a combination of factors including repeated behaviours, the vibe of physical spaces, cultural norms, brand personality, the pace of growth, collaborative habits, attitudes toward learning, diversity of experiences, and many other tangible and intangible elements that combine to determine the level and quality of organizational energy. Think WeWork or Nike versus General Motors or IBM. Think spunky start-up or passionate nonprofit versus "beige" insurance company or staid department store.

In *Free Time*, Jenny Blake describes the reciprocal relationship between personal and organizational energy. She affirms the importance of your work being life-giving, increasing your energy rather than taking it away. She describes energy as being more precious than money, so leaders need to be "mindful of preventing small, compounding withdrawals" from our bank accounts of energy and focus. She suggests that our "energetic fingerprints are embedded in every fibre of the final product."[49]

Kim Cameron unpacks this connection further in *Positively Energizing Leadership*, suggesting that the energy of the leader is an organization's strongest predictor of extraordinary outcomes, trumping all other factors.[50] He refers to the heliotropic principle, at the heart of much of positive psychology and Appreciative Inquiry: people move toward what gives them light and life. "Positive energizers" lift the performance of those around them. He refers to them as "incandescent people" and reports that the greatest predictor of success for leaders is "not their charisma, influence, or power. It is not personality, attractiveness, or innovative genius. The one thing that supersedes all these factors is positive relational energy: the energy exchanged between people that helps uplift, enthuse, and renew them." Unlike mental and physical energy, relational energy is self-renewing. It becomes reciprocal. Cameron calls this kind of energetic leadership an "active demonstration of values" that builds well-being and engagement, lowers turnover, and increases productivity and profitability. He refers to it as "the most underused yet powerful predictor of leadership and organizational success."[51]

How to amplify it

Since energy is most frequently thought of as an individual trait, advice for increasing it tends to be personal rather than collective. For example, in their profile of successful CEOs, McKinsey & Company writes about the importance of infusing energy into their routine as one way CEOs manage their personal effectiveness.[52] They refer to the importance of habits such as sufficient sleep, healthy nutrition, regular exercise, controlled stress, and disciplined calendar management to boost energy.[53] Rob Cross builds on this idea, suggesting that successful people have multidimensional lives that give them energy and pull them into a broader version of themselves.[54]

While these benefits are accurate, and a chronic lack of energy or depletion of one's regular energy level should be monitored as a sign of burnout,[55] I consider these personal habits as necessary but insufficient conditions for supporting what I'm describing as organizational energy. While leveraging our personal energy might be one step toward gains in personal productivity,[56] energy stewardship is not only an individual matter. Michael Watkins suggests that leadership is the ability to mobilize and focus potential energy to do desired work on a sustainable basis at individual, team, and systemic or organizational levels.[57]

One step toward guarding our energy is being mindful of it in the first place. In the workshops that contributed to this book, I asked participants what they most needed to do with their energy right now. Was it simply to pay attention to it? Was it to value it more highly? How about to recharge it, sustain it, or spread it? Perhaps it was to redirect it? Or reverse it from a negative tendency to a more positive orientation? The sample size was small, but the overwhelming response at that time was a need to recharge energy, as people were feeling quite depleted (midwinter in Canada during lockdown will have that effect on people!). It makes me curious how they might answer differently over time. Our energy needs shift, and we need to keep tabs on them so that we know which strategies to employ to keep our energy in a healthy state.

In *Competing in the New World of Work*, Keith Ferrazzi writes that for the sake of team resilience in the new world of work, monitoring each other's energy levels is now everyone's job.[58] He affirms what has long been my assertion: as leaders, we are in the business of group energy management. Ferrazzi asserts that energy comes from trust plus purpose. Leaders have an important role in earning the former and articulating the latter.

What are other pathways to increased collective energy? First, we need to choose to prioritize it. In his small but mighty book *Useful Beliefs*, Chris Helder asserts that energy is a decision.[59] We therefore must start by making the choice to give it our attention, since energy flows where our attention goes.[60] In assessing an organization's culture, Shane Hatton encourages us to pay attention to where the leader invests their energy, as it is an indicator of where their priorities lie.[61]

Next, do something. Energy is both a prerequisite and a result. Extraordinary results require big energy, but in turn, taking action builds energy. But not all "doing" is created equal when it comes to amplifying energy. As Jamie Gruman describes in *Boost*,[62] and Daniel Pink in *When*,[63] the type and timing of your activity matters. Not surprisingly, watching Netflix until the wee hours is not as energizing as going for a brisk morning walk in nature, for instance.

Focus also builds energy. In *The 4 Disciplines of Execution*, Sean Covey suggests that leaders should devote "disproportionate energy" to a very few things.[64] Similarly, in *Good Strategy Bad Strategy*, Richard Rumelt advises focusing energy and resources on very few pivotal objectives, whose accomplishment will lead to a cascade of favourable outcomes.[65] Like a laser cutter versus a traditional handsaw, focus concentrates our energy, thereby making it more powerful, without unnecessary force. As Diana Renner and Steven D'Souza remind us in *Not Doing*, you "cannot push water."[66] Energy should not be forced.

Making progress toward a goal builds energy because it stokes motivation. Progress is particularly motivating when it is linked to a shared view of a positive future, which *The Anticipatory Organization* by Daniel Burrus describes as building a sense of energy, empowerment, and a pervasive attention to the enormous opportunities in the days ahead.[67] It provides collective confidence that fosters bold moves.

An outward orientation of service to others and/or a bigger goal can also be energizing. Writing on servant leadership, pioneered by such authors as Robert Greenleaf and Ken Blanchard, points in this direction, as does more recent work in the field of psychological strain on leaders.[68] Jaquie Scammell asserts, "It is through great service that we can renew and sustain our energy."[69] Kim Cameron's work with positive energizers supports this finding. He identifies the core habits of positive energizers, and all of them are outward-focused. Positive energizers help other people to flourish. They express gratitude and humility. They instil a sense of confidence and self-efficacy in others. They listen actively and empathetically. They are trusting and trustworthy. And they motivate others to exceed performance standards rather than simply doing a job that is "good enough."[70]

Following through on our commitments is also a reliable source of energy. In his long-time bestseller *The Four Agreements*, Don Miguel Ruiz argues that the four agreements of being impeccable with your word, not taking anything personally, not making assumptions, and always doing your best break the power of behaviours that deplete our energy.[71]

Energy is both our fuel and our fuel gauge. Leaders are well-advised to pay attention to it in themselves and in others.

LIKEABILITY

Some cause happiness wherever they go;
others whenever they go.
~Oscar Wilde

What it is and why we need it

Positive energizers are likeable people.

Likeability may seem like a surprising quality to make this list of ELASTIC skills, and admittedly I have my reservations about including it.

Here's why it's here: a couple of years ago, I was preparing for a master-mind workshop with a small group of senior community leaders. We were planning to talk about being more persuasive. Leaders aren't leaders if they can't convince anyone to follow them, after all. As I researched the factors that contribute to persuasiveness, I was surprised to learn that one of the most powerful determinants of persuasiveness is likeability.

Consider the following examples.

- Jurors report finding likeable expert witnesses more persuasive than less likeable ones.[72]

- The more likeable a person recalls someone being, the more likely they are to change their attitude based on that person's message.[73]

- "Givers" are over-represented at the top of most measures of success and even tend to live longer.[74]

- Managing what your boss thinks of you is more impactful than your effort or performance. Flattery works even when your boss is aware you are being insincere.[75]

- "Not being nice may look promising at first, but in the long run it can destroy the very environment it needs for its own success."[76] Mean people need nice people, stability, and rules to make their meanness work!

- When you speak well of a person to someone else, that person transfers those positive traits to you.[77]

I looked at more than 20 other factors contributing to persuasive leadership, almost wishing this finding not to be true, and yet time and again the research and people's experience pointed to the importance of someone being likeable if they were going to persuade others to adopt their point of view or change their behaviour in a particular direction. Our reputation depends on how others perceive us to be treating them.

Being persuasive is closely related to having influence. In some contexts, "persuasive" and "influential" are synonyms. Historically, influence has frequently been attributed to a person's position or role, whereas persuasiveness seems to point more strongly to their compelling style or approach. It was in this latter category that likeability featured prominently (the two concepts also seem to blend in with the more modern incarnation of an "influencer"). Tom Peters identified being persuasive as part of the transition from employee to brand.[78]

Influential people stand out. They are more likely to command respect from colleagues and be noticed for opportunities.[79, 80, 81]

Commercial creativity leaders Kieran Flanagan and Dan Gregory argue in *Forever Skills*, "Ideas without influence are impotent."[82] They go on to assert that rarely does the best win, but rather the most influential. Even more provocatively, they suggest that relying on facts over influence can actually be counterproductive. This reminder aligns with much of what we know about purchasing decisions, that is, people make decisions based on emotions and justify them with facts. This emphasis on likeability as a leadership superpower taps into that emotional connection.

I had three related reasons for my hesitation in including likeability here. The first is related to power inequalities, particularly gender imbalances. Likeability is often equated with "niceness." Niceness is not a leadership quality I would espouse, and it is not applied to all genders equally. As Alicia Menendez has documented in *The Likability Trap*, pressure to be "nice" or "amiable" has been used as a societal expectation that keeps women's contributions and self-perceptions small.[83] This dynamic is exacerbated when gender is overlaid with ethnic or racial marginalization, or other layers of inequality. Warmth has been equated with weakness and even incompetence, while coldness is associated with strength.[84, 85, 86, 87]

The second reason is that likeability implies winning an invisible popularity contest. Just like on the playground where it can be difficult to discern why some people are "in" and others "out," likeability is strongly subject to various biases that may perpetuate the inequalities of the status quo, including cultural or gender-based discrimination. It can fortify an "old boys' club" or something similar. I find it difficult to write about it without falling into descriptions of likeability that match my own personal preferences and biases. It is well-proven that we tend to like those who are most like us. This familiarity bias is so powerful that Dr. Stephen Reysen includes it in his validated, 11-question Likability Scale, asking about the extent someone is similar to us as a measure of their likeability.[88]

The third reservation has to do with likeability lacking gravitas. It feels too light and superficial alongside heavyweight qualities such as adaptability and trust. Would we not rather include something with more substance, such as integrity or worthiness of respect? Dr. Reysen's Likability Scale also includes a question on attractive physical appearance; surely we would prefer to espouse something more deeply character-based? Is likeability a quality I would feel comfortable having included in my performance review?

The group involved in helping shape the material in this book, who met for a series of workshops through 2021 and 2022, held similar reservations to mine. Participants were almost split down the middle as to whether likeability should make the cut. As one person quipped, "Most con artists are likeable!" They craved something more akin to integrity or trustworthiness that reflected an alignment of deep values with another person. Nancy MacKay and Alan Weiss express it this way:

> "We want to be liked, and we want respect. But these aren't synonymous. This may seem jarring, but respect is far more important than affection in this work. It is helpful if people like us, but it is far more important that people respect us. I may like you, but I think you are giving me poor advice or poor direction. But if I respect you, I'm going to be much more prone to listen to and implement your suggestions and direction [...] I don't need to like the heart surgeon or the intellectual property attorney or the winning Super Bowl coach. I want to work with, play for, and trust the people who I respect."[89]

Even as I write this, I wonder if R for respect might have been more appropriate than L for likeable. However, not only does that ruin the acronym, it's also less specific. The research points specifically to likeability, and not just to respect which, although important enough to appear in many lists of corporate values, does not represent a set of behaviours that is uniformly understood or deemed as persuasive.

What the group did underline was that likeability is a composite measure of many other qualities. And those qualities might vary person-to-person not so much in the leader, but in the mind of the person doing the liking. The issue may not be to define the components of likeability in a universal way, but rather to highlight the importance of being perceived as likeable. Can we even know this about ourselves, let alone control it?

Sigh. Does a focus on likeability not lead us down a path of caring too much what other people think?

Reysen's Likability Scale provides one proven way to measure it, and thankfully it also assesses qualities such as friendliness, warmth, and approachability alongside appearance and familiarity. Likeable people are those you would choose to spend time with in a variety of contexts, for instance as a roommate, co-worker, or friend. You see them as know-ledgeable, and you would ask them for advice.[90]

Another meta-analysis of likeability identified seven traits that comprise it: friendliness, humour, happiness, kindness, positivity, tolerance, and honesty.[91]

We know from experience that likeability acts as a lubricant. If we want to get something done or ask a favour of someone, we are much more likely to go to the person with whom we have built strong relational currency. We also know that if we are applying for a job and we have the option of choosing colleagues with whom we already have strong rap-port, we are more likely to accept that job over another one where the people are unfamiliar or unpleasant. Chemistry is an intangible but highly important factor in our decision. You will become like the people you work with, far more likely than the other way around, so choose careful-ly.[92] We also know that if we are working together toward a tight deadline, we are more likely to work efficiently with a group we enjoy. Likeability smooths the way and helps get things done. It may even act as a buffer to compensate for bad behaviour or poor performance. For better or worse, we extend more grace to people we like.

Another sigh. Welcome to the territory of backroom handshake deals.

Thankfully, there is more to it. As early as 1959, John French and Bertram Raven coined the term "referent power," which has since been popularized by Ken Blanchard's situational leadership approach. Referent power stems from a leader's ability to inspire and influence others, based on the extent people admire, respect, and like that leader. It sits alongside but is separate from power that comes from expertise, position, or even charisma.[93] Building referent power is primarily about demonstrating interpersonal skills that create strong connections between a leader and their followers, where the leader serves as a positive, unifying, inspirational role model who promotes effective collaboration, productivity, and high morale.[94, 95]

Let's circle back to the notion of gravitas. What do we call likeability with substance? Someone can make a strong first impression with what we'll call "superficial likeability," but for that impression to hold up over time, likeability needs to be underpinned by a minimum standard of integrity and technical competence. As Bernard Marr writes, "No matter the organization or industry, everyone wants to work with a "loveable star" who combines competence and likeability."[96] We all want to collaborate with people who build rapport easily with us and whose presence we find uplifting. It helps to get things done, but it's not enough. Michael Port would agree. In his bestseller *Book Yourself Solid*, he writes about the importance of building both trust and credibility. One step toward those? "Become a likeable expert in your field."[97] "Tyrants and curmudgeons with brilliant vision can command a reluctant following for a time, but it never lasts."[98] Dr. Tomas Chamorro-Premuzic's summary of behaviours he calls "better than niceness at work" include being "rewarding to deal with" and demonstrating "organizational citizenship" as more proven pathways to a strong reputation.[99, 100] Likeable leaders have integrity, they are humble, they give time generously, they are steady, they form connections, they are positive, they listen, they are focused, they know how to have fun, they are honest, and they make mistakes. It's a category that goes far deeper than superficial agreeableness.

Likeability is also learnable, being linked to both emotional and social intelligence. Dr. Travis Bradberry affirms that likeability is under our control because it is directly linked to identifiable, measurable, and learnable behaviours, such as being approachable, even-keeled, generous, humble, encouraging, and perceptive.[101] Chris Voss refers to this combination of emotional intelligence plus influence as "tactical empathy."[102] Drawing on Dale Carnegie's 1937 *How to Win Friends and Influence People*, The Leadership Institute also highlights likeability as a learnable skill, identifying it as one of the top three areas where success as a leader is paramount.[103]

Yet we need to come at it indirectly. According to one workshop participant, "This concept is not about being liked, but about behaving in ways that make us likeable." Carey Nieuwhof concurs. He asserts that if you focus on being liked, you won't lead. Leadership requires you to take people to destinations they would not go without your leadership. You can lead and still be likeable, but it is a result rather than a goal.[104] Being likeable is not the same as being liked all of the time. It is more synonymous with being respected and respectable.[105]

How to amplify it

There is a growing body of evidence to support the importance of likeability in leadership. Let's explore how to strengthen it with three qualifiers in mind:

- Likeable people over the long term *are* trustworthy.
- Likeability is a skill that can be cultivated, more than an arbitrary or universal popularity contest.

LIKEABILITY

- Likeability may be a result of other traits rather than something to be worked on singularly and directly.

Writing on likeability tends to describe what it looks like more than how to grow it. Instead, I'd like to highlight some of the frequently recommended, practical, learnable interpersonal behaviours that lead to likeable qualities. Admittedly, in aggregate they sound like a call to "be a good human," but notice the powerful alchemy of an outward orientation combined with a commitment to standards that do not fluctuate based on others' opinions.[106, 107]

- Know and stick to what Ken Gosnell calls your "concrete guideposts."[108]

- Set what Jim Collins refers to as "inspired standards" rather than feeling you have to lead with an inspiring personality. It is more important to combine humility with a ferocious resolve.[109]

- Model the behaviours you want to see.

- Share information.

- Ask for what you want. As Vanessa Bohns underscores, we fail to appreciate the influence we already have. People want to help us more than we think![110]

- Admit when you are wrong or don't know something.

- Deliver on your promises.

- Accept feedback graciously and act on it.

- Add value.

- Be fair.

- Be curious about other people and listen well.

- Be diligent about acts of thoughtfulness.

- See the best in other people.

- Recognize good work.

- Keep learning.[111]

As Adam Grant reminds us, the person most likely to persuade you to change your mind is you![112] The ultimate benefit of likeability is becoming likeable to yourself. Like energy, it's both a precondition and a result. As much as likeability is about connecting well with other people, the time-honoured biblical command holds true: "Love your neighbour as yourself."

LIKEABILITY

ADAPTABILITY

The slowest piece of change you'll ever experience
for the rest of your life is happening right now.
~ Dan Gilbert

What it is and why we need it

When I first read that quote by Dan Gilbert in a book called *The Adaptation Advantage*[113] by Heather McGowan and Chris Shipley, it stopped me short. It was year one of the pandemic. It felt like the world had been turned upside down, I had no idea how much longer we would be living in lockdown, and my ability to cope with even faster change frankly seemed quite suspect at that time. Gilbert's assertion sent me on a journey of discovery, trying to find tangible ways to help my clients and myself keep up with the accelerating pace of change not only more effectively, but perhaps more willingly, or even joyfully.

We have frequently heard it said that the only constant is change. Having lived through the unprecedented global turbulence of recent years, you don't need me to tell you that adaptability is a relevant, necessary skill. The pace of change is increasing exponentially in many realms, and humans are struggling to keep up. As April Rinne, author of *Flux*,[114] asserts, "We need to reshape our relationship with change to be fit for a

world in flux. We need to be prepared for this sense of constant, sometimes relentless, change, much of which we can't control or we don't see
coming. And we need to figure out how we adapt to that."[115]

Adaptability is about being responsive in a generative way. It means
not just reacting to a new situation or freezing in the face of change, but
nimbly and productively adjusting as conditions shift. In her TED Talk on
adaptability, venture investor Natalie Fratto defines it as a must-have skill
that captures "how well a person reacts to the inevitability of change."[116]
While adaptability is frequently used synonymously with resilience,
resilience involves bouncing back, usually from adversity.[117] Adaptability
helps us "bounce forward" out of any kind of change. This involves not just
responding well to a challenge but thriving beyond it. Our typical, default
response to change is to react, cope, and conform; adaptability allows us
to embrace it and transform.[118]

McKinsey grounds this concept in learning, defining adaptability
as, "The ability to learn flexibly and efficiently and to apply that knowledge across situations." It is called a meta-skill of learning how to learn.
Improving our adaptability allows us to be faster and better at learning.
Adaptability is described as the critical success factor during periods of
transformation and systemic change.[119] It is not a trait, but a skill that can
be improved.

Adaptability is not just the ability to respond. It also involves a willingness to do so at a pace that is timely. This is why some definitions of adaptability refer not just to responding to change, but responding quickly to it.
For instance, Birkinshaw and Gibson define organizational adaptability
as, "The ability to move quickly toward new opportunities, to adjust to
volatile markets and to avoid complacency."[120] The same McKinsey report
cited above adds a second part to their definition of adaptability. It is
not only learning how to learn, but "being conscious of when to put that
learner's mind into action."[121]

Adaptability needs to happen in a timely way, but it also requires discernment to know when to pause. We cannot adapt effectively, constantly, uninterrupted, forever. Developing "absorptive capacity" is also critical, giving an organization and the individuals within it time to incorporate what's been tried and learned into existing practices and beliefs. We cannot keep adding and adding without an opportunity to integrate ideas and consciously decide what is worth keeping and what needs pruning. Birkinshaw and Gibson found that adaptability requires dynamic capabilities that "enable an organization to renew its competencies to achieve congruence with the changing environment," as well as operational capabilities and absorptive capacity in high-velocity environments.[122] A lack of time to absorb is likely why the word "pivot" became such a lightning rod in the early days of the pandemic. I heard more than one client exclaim with frustration, "No one uses the word 'pivot' in this room today!"

Similarly, adaptability is not something that can occur in all domains simultaneously. As previously described, elasticity requires some fixed points. In turbulent times, we may have felt that everything was changing at once, but in fact some things did stay the same. For example, how we obtained our groceries likely changed during the pandemic, but the need to buy food did not. How we educated or cared for our children at times shifted, but the need to arrange childcare did not. Many activities that we enjoyed pre-pandemic remained accessible during the pandemic, such as hiking or board games or jigsaw puzzles or, for me, knitting. It is helpful to identify those elements that are not changing in order to maintain the capacity to change in other ways.

Kelly McGonigal's research on willpower is interesting in this regard. She explores evidence showing that when we need to exercise self-control or focus our energies in one area, it leaves little battery life left to concentrate in other areas. Self-discipline is a zero-sum game.[123] Thus, although we can increase our overall capacity to adapt over time, adapting in one area may leave us with little energy to adapt in another until we take time

ADAPTABILITY

to recharge. It has been my experience that in times of major disruption, what is fixed in our lives can change, but the need to have some things remain fixed does not. If every point is moving at once, there is no stretch. We therefore need to understand the areas in which we are not changing, in order to enable change in the areas where we most need to adapt.

It should come as no surprise that adaptability features near the top of every current list of future employability skills.[124] Adaptability is a trait that every employer should be looking for. We know we need it. The question is: how do we recognize it and/or grow it? Is adaptability something leaders can teach and model, spot in others, and strengthen, like a muscle or a skill? Or is it more of a temperament trait that a person is either born with or they aren't? Or something we all do, like breathing, such that it is not a useful leadership differentiator at all?

Adaptability is a learnable skill that can yield sustainable change. It is not an easy skill—even for the most successful among us—but it can be nurtured with continual practice.[125] Adaptability is difficult to master, in part because we tend to actively resist doing so. The same elements that make adaptability so necessary may also trigger fear in us, making us default to familiar patterns. "We resist the change we can't control—the change that blindsides us, the change that goes against our expectations, the change that delays our plans or disrupts them entirely."[126]

The rewards of increasing adaptability are worth the effort: companies with strong cultures that emphasize adaptability turn in better financial performance. Higher levels of adaptability are associated with greater levels of learning ability and better performance, confidence, and creative output. Adaptability is also crucial for psychological and physical well-being and is linked to higher levels of social support and overall life satisfaction.[127] People with high adaptability scores are energized by the need to adapt.

Much like energy, adaptability is commonly thought of as an individual skill. For instance, McKinsey identifies adaptability as one skill of high performing CEOs in a section called *managing personal effectiveness*.[128] While it is true that we often need to adapt personally, our environments enable or inhibit that from happening. Organizations need to develop a culture and set of skills that allow for corporate nimbleness and agility. Gibson defines organizational adaptability as, "The ability to move quickly toward new opportunities, to adjust to volatile markets and to avoid complacency."[129]

How to build it

With new tools available to measure adaptability[130], we are in a stronger position than ever before to improve it empirically at both personal and corporate levels.

Before diving into specifics of how to do that, it is useful first to identify your philosophy of improvement. Once you know your adaptability "score," do you intend to fortify existing areas of strength and/or shore up areas of vulnerability? Particularly for the high achievers among us, negativity bias is strong. That means that we tend to over-index on the negative. Perhaps you received a stellar report card in school, but ruminated on the one grade that was not as high as the others, or the one phrase in the comments that was not as glowing. We give negative data disproportionate attention.

In my adaptability coaching practice, I try to offset this tendency by inviting clients to amplify their strengths, as those areas represent our preferred pathways to adapting. We will be more impactful if we leverage existing strengths, in part because it is easier for us to follow paths in which we are already strong. This appreciative approach is borne out in approaches such as Appreciative Inquiry, Strengthsfinder, and positive psychology. Improving in an area where I am already strong will allow me to enjoy the process and to stand out even more having made that improvement.

Because adaptability comprises multiple factors, it can be nurtured in numerous ways. [131]For example, the strategies one might use to nurture grit will be different than those used to strengthen team support, but each will contribute to stronger adaptability overall.

We can begin to strengthen our adaptability first by setting expectations. "Expectation has a striking capacity to shape experience."[132] For instance, if we accept that there is no steady state or endgame, we will be more prepared to adapt continually.[133]

Next, practise seeing the world through an adaptability lens, not just through default mindsets and behaviours. McKinsey describes this lens as having multiple dimensions including curiosity, creativity, self-awareness, and a growth mindset.[134] Becoming conscious of the area we would like to change is a first step toward making that happen.

Because there are dispositional, cognitive, behavioural, and emotional elements to adaptability, it can be improved through a range of behavioural, cognitive, and coaching strategies. Behavioural strategies could include: active coping habits that reduce fear and stress responses; boosting physical health through sleep, good nutrition, and exercise; and strengthening social support and connections through close, meaningful relationships and gratitude. The link between adaptability and building deeper and more diverse connections with people is perhaps unexpectedly strong. These relationships build our skills of attention, vulnerability, empathy, and compassion, which are pathways to greater adaptability. They open us to new perspectives and reduce confirmation bias.[135, 136, 137]

Cognitive strategies could include learning stronger emotional regulation skills such as acceptance, affect labelling, expression, and reframing; learning about the plasticity of the brain; intentionally building our curiosity; and cognitive training through practices such as mindfulness or therapy.

Coaching can facilitate behaviour change through broadening our repertoire of thriving strategies and getting useful feedback as we do.

ADAPTABILITY

These strategies could include building self-belief, a sense of safety, and/ or confidence in the efficacy of an intervention. Some are known to have an outsized effect of boosting the effectiveness of other ones. Well-being as a practice is one such disproportionately foundational skill, as our physical and mental health are both preconditions and accelerants to adaptability.[138, 139]

Todd Henry calls adaptability "the key counterpoint to ego." He highlights the importance of maintaining a strong sense of self and purpose while confidently bending to your environment.[140] Adaptability requires staying anchored to deep values and long-terms aims to help us stay appropriately responsive.

The need to adapt can cause our identities to be disrupted. Thus, rather than tying ourselves to, for example, our job title or even a specific professional category, McCowan and Shipley suggest "[Tethering] yourself in future stories."[141] In The Willpower Instinct, Kelly McGonigal suggests that our future self can feel like a stranger.[142] We need to get to know her, such that the future feels vivid and real. Vividness is an extremely advanced form of connection with our future self. As Ben Hardy writes in Be Your Future Self Now, the quality of connection we have to our future self-determines the quality of our life and behaviours now. He cites Dr. Roy Baumeister and Dr. Kathleen Vohs, who argue that "Present events draw meaning from their connection to future outcomes."[143]

Flanagan and Gregory highlight that resilience is really mental agility, as we must reframe our experience in the face of setbacks and changing conditions, not just repeat the same failed strategies.[144] Thus, adaptability requires creativity, so it will be strengthened when our creativity improves.

We also know that adaptability is a function of our environments.[145] Thus, embracing new situations, working in inspiring or unfamiliar settings, and seeking to create more innovative cultures can feed both organizational and personal adaptability.[146] Keith Ferrazzi's research suggests

ADAPTABILITY

that teams' strong adaptability under adverse conditions has much to do with the healthy behavioural norms and strong working relationships within those teams. Shared purpose then functions as a "force multiplier for radical adaptability."[147]

Adaptability is fundamentally about learning to learn. We must therefore create environments where it is safe to learn.[148] Because internal mobility has become a higher priority for workers over the past few years, rapid upskilling is key to taking on emerging roles.[149, 150] We need to practise learning new skills at pace.

It helps to remember that what worked in our past may not work in the future.[151] Unlearning is therefore as critical to adaptability as learning. Unlearning requires recognizing that doing what brought you success in the past won't necessarily deliver the same results. It requires consciously letting go of once-useful mindsets and behaviours, both to make space for and to limit resistance to new ways of doing things.[152] This skill of overwriting old data with new is useful both personally and organizationally. Gary Hamel suggests looking for enemies of adaptability and rooting them out.[153]

Uhl-Biena and Arenab argue that a focus on organizational performance will not necessarily make that organization more adaptable.

> "Leadership for organizational adaptability is different from
> traditional leadership or leading change. It involves enabling
> the adaptive process by creating space for ideas advanced
> by entrepreneurial leaders to engage in tension with the
> operational system and generate innovations that scale into
> the system to meet the adaptive needs of the organization and
> its environment. Leadership for organizational adaptability
> calls for scholars and practitioners to recognize organizational
> adaptability as an important organizational outcome, and
> enabling leadership (i.e., enabling the adaptive process

ADAPTABILITY

through adaptive space) as a critical form of leadership for
adaptive organizations."[154]

Leaders need to create adaptive spaces for conflicting and connecting. These are different from entrepreneurial or operational spaces. Key leadership roles of the future will look different than in the past, and will include brokering, energizing, facilitating, and connecting.[155]

Taking action, of almost any kind, is motivating, and practice helps. Edgar Schein encourages us to identify our "next adaptive move," describing it as usually quick, small, and counterintuitive.[156] As we practise, obstacles will undoubtedly arise. I am encouraged by the words of Marcus Aurelius (from the year 170 AD!), quoted by modern philosopher Ryan Holiday: "Our actions may be impeded... but there can be no impeding our intentions or dispositions. Because we can accommodate and adapt. The mind adapts and converts to its own purposes the obstacle to our acting. [...] The impediment to action advances action. What stands in the way becomes the way."[157]

Similarly, practising simulations that help us think of solutions can strengthen our adaptability muscle. Natalie Fratto suggests posing "What if?" questions and coming up with solutions, as well as actively exploring and seeking unfamiliar opportunities.[158, 159] Her suggestions are echoed by Keith Keating, who recommends planning for multiple scenarios as an adaptable leader, not primarily in order to be accurate in our predictions, but rather because planning creates focus.[160] Focus, if directed appropriately, perhaps unexpectedly contributes to our adaptability as it helps us remember what is critically important and what can be adjusted.

Because adaptability is like a muscle, perhaps these past years have allowed us to warm it up, and now it is time to actively put it to positive work. "The pandemic has proven we can be adaptable, even creative in a crisis. Now, let's get more ambitious. Let's apply that creativity and our

ADAPTABILITY

ability to pull together to start boldly planning for longer-term success, despite uncertainty."[161]

And perhaps we can consider surpassing adapting, toward transforming. In *The Power of Onlyness*, Nilofer Merchant laments that we are more likely to adapt to a context than dent it.[162] What if we endeavoured instead to make our dent?

ADAPTABILITY

STRATEGY

*"Building a visionary company requires
1% vision and 99% alignment."*
~Jim Collins and Jerry Porras[163]

What it is and why we need it

Strategic thinking is both a skill and a task. It is often equated with strategic planning (consult my book *Sightline* if you are interested in the mechanics of how to facilitate a collaborative strategic planning process).[164] But the strategic skill I am exploring here, while useful in strategic planning, is not synonymous with it. Here, I am probing the mindset or skillset of a leader who maintains a strategic point of view.

Strategic is a word that is often used and rarely defined. It is usually used rather loosely to mean the opposite of tactical or "in the weeds." Sometimes it means something more character-based such as shrewd or wise. Here, "strategic" refers to someone who can see a big picture and take a long-term view, and link that broader perspective to day-to-day decisions and instructions. Strategy involves an ability to see how a desired future connects to the here and now.[165] It is an inherently social task, as it requires bringing others along with you, to see a collective vision and to help execute it.

A strategic leader can do what a mentor of mine calls "look down the long road" and lift others' gaze to do the same, even in the midst of daily demands. They cast a vision of a desired future and convey hope that getting there is possible. In *Go for Bold*, Rosie Yeo describes the three components of strategy as a great idea, a clear pathway, and a shared story.[166] Strategy is about mapping a coherent route to an objective.[167] Strong leaders must be strategists.

Some understandings of strategy incorporate execution, since a strategy that is not implemented is little more than an idea. For instance, in the *Strategy Safari*, Henry Mintzberg and his co-authors define strategic thinking as being about both seeing—ahead, behind, up, down, beside, above, below, beyond—and seeing it through.[168] Strategic leaders create and express vision, and drive it through to completion. Similarly, Richard Rumelt in *The Crux*, describes strategic skill as having three parts: judgement about which issues are truly important and about the difficulties of dealing with those issues, and the ability to focus on the crux—the most important part of a set of challenges that has a good chance of being solved by coherent action.[169]

Being strategic does not require you to be clairvoyant. I've written about this before and it bears repeating because, particularly after our collective experience of uncertainty through COVID 19, I have witnessed an intense reluctance to plan because the world is so uncertain. People are more unsure than ever about their ability to see around the next bend, and as a result they swing toward not planning at all. But strategy is less about prediction and more about informed anticipation. It is about developing the habit of foreseeing what might reasonably be coming without requiring accurate predictions as a precondition for strategic success. It is a tricky balance.

Strategy compels us to look ahead while remaining open to the likelihood that the future will be different than we expect. The accuracy of our predictions matters less than the practice and discipline of noticing what is happening around us when it comes to strengthening our strategy muscles. As Daniel Burrus argues in *The Anticipatory Organization*, it is strategically critical to be able to recognize and differentiate between the types of trends shaping your environment.[170] Strategy helps us to pay attention.

If your organization manages to strategize effectively in seasons of uncertainty, it will stand out. As Alan G. Lafley and Roger Martin assert in *Playing to Win*, "Not only is strategy possible in times of tumultuous change, but it can be a competitive advantage and a source of significant value creation."[171]

Being truly strategic requires an impeccable sense of timing. When we feel the need to act quickly, resisting the pressure to act may be the best strategy, even if everything within us is pushing for an immediate response.[172] In *The Long Game*, Dorie Clark advocates for "strategic patience."[173] She suggests taking a "generational view," not just for multi-generational sustainability and stewardship, but because everything takes longer than we expect. Big goals are, by definition, usually impossible to achieve in the short term.

Being strategic also calls you to be brave. High-performing CEOs are characterized by their willingness to make big moves early and often. "You can't cross a chasm in two small jumps."[174]

It also requires you to be selective. Dorie Clark suggests over-indexing on a particular goal for a period of time and Oliver Burkeman is a fan of "strategic underachievement" that invites us to decide in advance what to fail at, since we cannot succeed at everything.[175, 176] Writing a book may be a good example of this. It is a strategic choice for me to put this book out in the world in order to expand my practice and be of service. But getting it written has required over-indexing on authoring for the summer of 2022, and consciously choosing to let my facilitation practice lie largely dormant for that time. You may also have experienced this if you've ever had a new baby. Your family over-indexes on keeping the small person alive

STRATEGY

and healthy, consciously (albeit with some frustration!) letting your personal fitness or the cleanliness of your house slide, hopefully temporarily.

Strategy should be an enabler of action, not a barrier to it. It serves as a filter for saying a clear defensible 'no' alongside an enthusiastic 'yes' to the opportunities that align with our aims. But while decisiveness can be an admirable strategic quality of leaders, increasingly they need to be clear about what is prescriptive in advance versus which choices can be made responsively in real time. To do that, leaders must develop the skill of discerning and then communicating what is fixed and what is flexible (I'm sure this theme is sounding familiar by now!).

Fixed elements in strategy usually involve things like organizational mission, values, and principles that guide ways of working together. They might also include identifying which problems our strategy will solve. It's been my experience that the list of fixed elements is shorter than we might once have thought. Which means that many other elements of strategy are sorted out in the moment rather than in advance. I think of it as having strong clarity about where you are heading, but enormous flexibility about how to get there. Consider the analogy of a road trip. You know your ultimate destination, but might be open to taking the scenic route at times, coping with construction and road closures as needed, or delighting in finding a newly paved superhighway that cuts time off your drive during the boring patches. You are not adamant before you leave about the precise route you will take to get there or the exact time of arrival, but even amongst the detours, your eventual destination remains clear.

The field of emergent strategy has been articulated best by adrienne maree brown. She draws on a definition of emergence from Nick Obolensky: "Emergence is the way complex systems and patterns arise out of a multiplicity of relatively simple interactions."[177] Emergent strategy is adaptive, not linear. It involves remembering that change is constant and that the large is a reflection of the small; finding the

STRATEGY

conversation that only these people in this moment can have; trusting there is always enough time for the right work; moving at the speed of the relationship; amplifying presence; and remembering that what you pay attention to grows.[178] She suggests the more ease and intention we bring to change, the more change can serve our vision.[179] Increasingly, even more traditional strategists are acknowledging the messiness of the practice and the need to be more adaptive than technical, guided more by values and principles than rigid goals.[180]

Strategy development is best done collaboratively, which also requires strategic leadership and facilitation. A collective experience creates opportunities to reach shared, powerful agreements about a team's long game. Rosie Yeo describes it this way: "When we create strategy together, we understand and feel ownership of the story and responsibility for achieving the outcome. Often this enables us to make bolder decisions, because we've worked through the risks together and understand the decisions in the context of our full story."[181]

Lafley and Martin concur: "Any new strategy is created in a social context [...] strategy requires a diverse team with the various members bringing their distinct perspectives to bear on the problem. A process for working collaboratively on strategy is essential because all companies are social entities."[182] Keith Ferrazzi highlights the particular importance of strategic alignment in this new age of remote work.[183]

Collective strategic thinking is worth the effort. It leads to a team that is informed and invested, an organization that is more credible and accountable, priorities that are focused and aligned, and decisions that are responsive and intentional.

Strategic leadership becomes evident when leaders leverage opportunities that others don't see. You witness strategic thinking at work in relationships that accelerate missional progress. Perhaps you have worked for someone who managed to develop partnerships well ahead of when they seemed to be needed. Yet when the time came, they had

STRATEGY

the relationships in place to make an amazing impact. It reminds me of real-estate developers who have the foresight to build infrastructure before houses are built such that when urban sprawl happens, they are ready to serve the burgeoning population. David Nour asserts, "The most important person in the next 10 years of your life, you haven't met yet!" He is an active proponent of investing proactively in strategic relationships to personal and professional growth.[184] That is a strategic leadership skill.

It turns out that strategic thinking is hard to come by. Based on a 2015 PwC study, just 8% of 6,000 senior leaders were found to be "strategists" who could solve wicked problems. That number had stayed roughly stable over the ten previous years. Interestingly, those few strategist leaders were more likely to be older women. The researchers describe them this way:

> "They can challenge the prevailing view without provoking outrage or cynicism; they can act on the big and small pictures at the same time, and change course if their chosen path turns out to be incorrect; and they lead with inquiry as well as advocacy, and with engagement as well as command, operating all the while from a deeply held humility and respect for others."[185]

In *The Long Game*, Dorie Clark reports that 97% of leaders say strategic thinking is key to their organization's success, but 96% claim they don't have enough time for long-term strategic thinking.[186] Yet our values play out in our behaviours. We make time for what is truly important to us. Jenny Blake encourages leaders to prioritize strategic thinking in this way: "Create more containers, within your golden hour windows, for strategic thinking. This is a 'do not pass go' moment! You will never free your time if you leave it to chance."[187]

STRATEGY

How to get good at it

The skills of a strategic leader do not always align with what people tend to get rewarded or promoted for. It is common for someone to be given more responsibility when their technical/operational skills are strong. These people then find themselves near the top of the organizational hierarchy, responsible for strategy but having had limited training or experience in it.

A review of the research on how to be a better strategic leader yields surprisingly little. Strategy development is an under-researched field in academia. In popular business literature, more is written about strategic plan development than strategic leadership. The lists of tips or qualities are generic, once again falling into the category of "be a decent human" rather than advice specifically directed at building strategic competencies. For example, several articles suggested approaches such as "communicate effectively" or "stay current," "delegate tasks" or "ask good questions." I can't disagree with any of these behaviours, but if someone were to do them all faithfully, would it make them a strategic leader at the end of the day? Not necessarily. I understand the challenge here. I appreciate the candour of one author who said, "Strategic leaders are often described as people who 'get it.'"[188] Not exactly specific or easily teachable, but the description resonates nonetheless.

Here are some proven behaviours which, taken together, will move you in the direction of being a more strategic leader:[189, 190, 191]

- Read widely and maintain a diverse network of contacts. Exposure to multiple perspectives helps to maintain a big picture and long-term view. Surround yourself with insightful people who will go deep with you and tell you the truth as they see it. Be open to others who challenge longstanding organizational behaviours that could stand to be disrupted.

STRATEGY

- Set aside time for learning and reflection. Dorie Clark writes about the importance of "creating white space" in order to play a longer game.[192]

- Make a habit of balancing present and future thinking.

- Develop a culture of adaptation and innovation inside which to embed strategy. Our environment can act as a powerful accelerant or obstacle to the behaviours we wish to amplify, so pay attention to aligning culture with strategic intents.[193] Build what Rosie Yeo calls a "collective strategic mindset."[194] Create processes that encourage experimentation so that new ideas can be tested in relatively low-risk ways.

- Be clear on the filters you will use to distill information. Without a clear rubric or sense of what is most important, you might drown in distraction.

- Maintain contact with frontline realities so you can connect your long-range vision with real-life operations. As leaders move up the organizational hierarchy, they tend to lose contact with shifting conditions on the frontlines, but rarely recognize that loss.

- Maintain a sense of timing. Big things often take longer than we expect. We do not always see the results of our labour in the short term. Dorie Clark recommends "keeping the faith" over the long haul.[195] Knowing when to stay the course and when to change direction requires discernment and patience. That pace is generally set by senior leaders.

TRUST

The best way to find out if you can trust
somebody is to trust them.
~Ernest Hemingway

What it is and why we need it

Trust is a quality that is overmentioned and underexplained. It appears in countless leadership books and lists of corporate values and is widely recognized as a precondition for solid teamwork. It is so ubiquitous that I hesitated to include it here. Remember, this is an acronym of compelling leadership qualities that are frequently overlooked, and surely trust is mentioned often enough not to make that list! Yet it is rarely unpacked in any detail.

Trust is useful. Simon Sinek likens it to lubrication, since it reduces friction and creates conditions more conducive to performance.[196] Amy Cuddy calls trust "The conduit of influence."[197] In that sense, trust resembles likeability. In his work on the importance of good process, Joel Brockner identifies trust as the mediating factor that allows us to get less bent out of shape at bad outcomes.[198] In sports, trust in leadership is both a determinant and a product of team performance.[199] People who trust others easily even make more money![200]

Yet trust is more than a nice-to-have. It is a must-have. Its importance is deeply intuitive.[201] I tend to put trust in the same category as personal integrity—someone is trusted if they follow through on their word. This level of integrity strikes me as the minimum requirement, barely even worth mentioning. It's been said if there is no trust problem, trust doesn't come up: "Strong teams don't even talk about [trust], but it dominates the conversation in struggling teams."[202] I prefer to work with strong teams—can we not therefore treat trust as a given and move on? Not so fast. Integrity, or what Simon Sinek refers to as "no ethical fading" is a minimum requirement or a necessary condition for trust, but perhaps not a sufficient one.[203] It does not take us far enough for trust to qualify as an ELASTIC leadership skill.

In developing this acronym, trust elicited curiosity in me, because I think there is more to it than what I've recently read. Trust tends to be seen in binary terms—it is either intact or broken, present or absent. It is rarely described as dynamic, contextual, or as a skill available to be developed. It is also assumed (including often by me) to be like table stakes; a non-negotiable, necessary condition for other things to happen. It is described as something that is slow to build but quick to erode. Are these assumptions accurate? Although much has been written on behaviours that build or erode trust, I was interested more specifically in whether it is possible to build trust quickly, at the pace of real life in the world of work.

I tend to treat trust as synonymous with being "trustworthy." But trust as a leadership skill also involves being both trusted and trusting. A leader who exemplifies trust is not just a person of integrity (who is "trustworthy"), but someone who is trusted and who extends trust. Herein lies a superpower of an ELASTIC leader. They don't just warrant trust; they actually get and give it.

Let's unpack this a bit further.

TRUST

Perhaps, like me, you have had a conversation with a teenager that goes something like this:

> Parent: Sets a boundary the teen doesn't like (think curfew or use of the car).
> Teen: "Why don't you trust me?"
> Parent: "I trust you with some things but not everything, and not yet with this thing."

Trust is contextually specific, not generally applicable in every situation. You might trust your eight-year-old not to touch the stove when it is hot, but you would not give them the keys to your car. You might trust your 17-year-old with your car, but you may not leave them home alone for a long weekend quite yet. Just as our children mature in their ability to be trusted, so too does trust get built over time in other relationships, including at work. While it is true that trust is earned, that happens not just over time but across skills and contexts.

But there are situations where someone might be trustworthy, at the level of character or skill, but not yet trusted at the level of behaviour or responsibility. They have not been given opportunities to prove their trustworthiness. Back to our conversation:

> Teen: "How will you know if I can be trusted with this specific thing if you never give me a chance to prove to you that I can be?"

Touché.

Can you hear (and feel) how trust is not just a cognitive, rational concept but also an emotional, relational one? It lights up the limbic part of our brain, which is our emotional centre.[204]

TRUST

In her poem *trust the people*, adrienne maree brown writes, "trust the people and you will become trustworthy."[205]

Being trusted is incredibly motivating. As Stephen M.R. Covey has said, "Trust lifts energy."[206] He refers to trust as the ultimate human currency, asserting that most people can and want to be trusted. Is trust risky? Perhaps, but Covey writes, "I prefer to give my trust a hundred times and risk being disappointed two or three times than to live perpetually in an atmosphere of distrust."[207]

Trust is a magnet for talent. People do their best work when they are trusted. Covey suggests that creating a high-trust culture to attract, engage, retain, and inspire talent is an "epic imperative" of all organizations today.[208] Marcus Buckingham refers to trust as a team's most valuable asset, because teams that trust each other are more engaged and resilient.[209] Not only is trust a positive force, but a lack of it is assertively negative. Bad behaviour is infectious, and expecting others to be untrustworthy is a self-fulfilling prophecy.[210] Therefore, trust is worthy of pursuit and a lack of it should be actively avoided.

Trust is a verb, not just a noun. It is something effective teams <u>do</u>. They extend and receive trust. Can you hear how this action orientation takes us to a different place than perceiving trust primarily as a static and passive character trait? "Think of what you would gain if your people trusted you more."[211]

Like energy, trust is often seen as personal more than institutional.[212] Although brands can become trusted over time, it is more difficult to imagine those brands extending trust. One possible example would be clothing brands such as Lululemon, Patagonia, Eddie Bauer, Nordstrom and others who are known for accepting returns of their merchandise, no questions asked. Is that corporate trust being extended to its customers?

"Without trust we have no speed."[213, 214] Trust moves at the speed of relationships and vice versa, but that speed is not necessarily slow. Trust can be built surprisingly quickly when shared anchor points are present. Trust is expedited when values and objectives align, with mutual likeability again acting as an accelerant.

But what if those multiple shared anchor points simply aren't there? In *Collaborating with the Enemy*, Adam Kahane asserts that progress is still possible where trust and agreement are low.[215] It starts with adjusting our expectations toward moments of both conflict and connection in the messy world of complexity. There is no one version of what is going on, and therefore no agreement on the problem, the solution or the plan. In that case, he suggests experimenting our way forward, likening the process to multiple teams rafting on a river versus one team following a map. He suggests that it is more important to act than to agree, quoting a former mayor of Bogota, Colombia who said, "The most robust agreements are those that different actors support for different reasons."

How to build it

Trust is often earned in small, repeated examples of delivering on your promises. I am reminded of a story shared by Walter Wangerin Jr in his book *As for Me and My House* that I read in the early 1990s and have called to mind often since.[216] Wangerin and his wife were going through a rocky patch in their marriage. In an effort to make amends, he promised to make himself available to talk to her every day. At that time, she was not in the mood to talk to him very much. But Wangerin knew how important it was to rebuild trust by following through on his commitment. So, every day at the agreed-upon time, he would sit on a stool in the kitchen while his wife made supper. He showed up for a bunch of days, and she didn't talk at all for that same bunch of days. It wasn't her reaction that was the main lesson; it was his repeated action that he carried out because he said he would. As she began to be able to trust that he would show up

TRUST

on that stool, conversation gradually began to flow and, slowly, healing happened. Trust can require mundane faithfulness.

Yet there is an ironic chicken-and-egg quality to trust—it needs to be extended before it can be earned. How the sentence "I will trust you to..." gets finished gradually grows in scope over time.

The notion of vulnerability between people as a reciprocal pathway to building trust between them has risen to prominence in recent years, most notably because of the fine work of Dr. Brené Brown.[217, 218] Empirical evidence suggests that while vulnerability is an important precondition to trust, the path to trust does not start there. The first step is competence. As with likeability, we initially need confidence that a person is capable, not clueless, before we will trust them. Flanagan and Gregory identify trust as a "forever skill." They define trust as an ability to rely on the knowledge and word of another person, to see them as an expert. Trust "shapes and is informed by our reputation."[219] That reputational currency is built through a combination of experience, track record, training, and responsibility.[220]

Competence is then followed by an increase in warmth. This is where you might notice considerable overlap between trust and likeability. We tend to trust people with whom we share a relationship, a history, and characteristics in common. Trust comes more easily with people we view as similar to us (I hope your red flags are beginning to fly—as with likeability, by prioritizing trust, do we risk unwittingly eroding a commitment to inclusion, diversity, and equity because we default to the status quo? Hmm...). Chris Voss sees this insight as something to be exploited in high-stakes negotiations, for example, because intentionally building a sense of similarity creates bridges between the parties.[221] His perspective is echoed by Harvard negotiation instructor Deepak Malhotra: "They need to like you."[222]

This sense of warmth and rapport is then followed by vulnerability, the cumulative effect of which is trust.

Imagine if someone you've never met or barely knew was to approach you in tears and reveal some of their most intimate secrets in public. Would you feel honoured, or more likely uncomfortable? I suspect you can viscerally feel what that is like—vulnerable yes, but also inappropriate and odd. Contrast this with the person whom you've come to know as reliable and capable in their job. You have built rapport through warm, friendly interactions over time. If that person were to come to you teary and vulnerable, the bond that will be created between you will strengthen your relationship in the future rather than making it increasingly awkward. In my experience, the sequence of that relationship building feels right. The first tip then is to get the order right.

Edgar Schein asserts that even though we know we work better with people we know and trust, people are rarely willing to invest in building that relationship.[223] Building trust takes relational investment.

Much writing on building trust in the workplace focuses on communication habits. Engage authentically with people. Align your words and actions. Listen more, talk less. Give and receive feedback. Demonstrate appreciation. [224,225]

Another contributor to trust at work has been identified by Joel Brockner as "high process fairness." When people feel they can trust the process by which a decision has been made, they are more likely to accept the decision, even when its consequences might be unfavorable to them.[226] Trust, therefore, is not just built between people but can be strengthened by processes and policies that support it.

The behaviours that build trust within organizations are the very behaviours that help to manage change. They are reciprocal and usually incremental. But according to the Centre for Creative Leadership, they are also often paradoxical because they require balancing both structures and people.[227] Consider the need to balance urgency with patience, optimism with realism, toughness with empathy, catalyzing change with coping with transition. A trusting and trusted leader learns how to

TRUST

navigate such tensions skilfully without needing to resolve them fully in one direction or the other.

Given its foundational, necessary quality, perhaps trust (receiving and extending) needs to be one of the fixed anchor points of ELASTIC leadership. When we've been stretched too far, we find our way back to values and people we trust. May we find that for ourselves and embody it for those we lead.

IMAGINATION

As imagination bodies forth the form of things unknown,
the poet's pen turns them to shape and gives to airy nothing
a local habitation and a name.
~Shakespeare

What it is and why we need it

You have arrived at the reason I wrote this book in the first place. Imagination, more specifically collective imagination, was my starting point for this exploration. While many of my clients have been touting evidence-based decision-making for a long time, and demonstrating experience-based decision-making much of the time, I find myself increasingly interested in supplementing those data sources with future-oriented descriptions of the new places they want their organizations to go. The latter is a creative task that requires exercising imagination rather than analysis. As Rosie Yeo rightly expresses it, "Strategy requires both information and imagination."[228] We know that "More data doesn't usually lead to better decisions"[229]—but what does? I suspect better facilitation, but also more imagination would help.

Even as I am drawn to this idea, I can feel resistance to it too, likely rooted in attending too many strategy retreats early in my career that involved flaky facilitators and the phrases "blue-sky thinking" and "every idea is a good idea." Imagination brings with it a tension between having no boundaries and needing them. Creativity thrives within constraints.

Imagination is not something frequently discussed in organizational literature, although it does appear in educational research at times.[230] As with other elements in the ELASTIC acronym, it is mentioned far more than it is analyzed. It is a bit mysterious. It still seems to be viewed as the territory of children or perhaps artists, but not serious thinkers. Organizations struggle to be imaginative; I suspect they rarely see it as a skill that belongs in their toolbox.

Martin Reeves and Jack Fuller describe it this way: "Imagination lies between perception and dreaming. It loosens the correlation to reality without cutting ties with it."[231] Notice the echoes with strategy—linking what is with what could be.

Imagination can be unruly. Yet traditional management is still mostly about control, preferring certainty and efficiency. Most imaginative or novel ideas won't work. How do we measure the return on investment of those? We find ourselves in a paradox: society needs new ideas in order to progress, so it has to find a way to get people to pursue new ideas, even though they may be mostly off-track, and it has to recognize that for most people, pursuing novel ideas is a bad idea.[232]

Imagination is frequently seen as an individual cognitive pursuit, happening only inside people's heads. It is rarely conceived as a group activity. Yet it is also interpersonal. Despite the pervasiveness of the image of the lone genius, empirical research confirms that ideas evolve socially, accelerated exponentially in recent times by our ability to share research findings and ideas globally almost instantaneously. Eric Weiner's work on the *Geography of Genius*[233] and Linda Hill et al.'s on *Collective Genius*[234] are both fascinating and instructive in pointing to the social nature of creativity. Even more recently, the global race to develop a vaccine against COVID 19 provides a powerful case study of collaborative innovation in real time.

IMAGINATION

Have you had the experience of looking to buy a particular car, then seeing that car on every road? I am reminded of British scientist Mary Leakey's observation: "You only find what you are looking for, really, if the truth be known." Collective imagination has become like that for me. The more attention I pay to it, the more essential it becomes in my leadership thinking. Groups of people need tools to see things in new ways.

I have been asked what differentiates imagination from the more commonly understood corporate terms of vision or innovation. My answer is that creativity and innovation require bringing something into being that wasn't there before. They are physical processes, whereas imagination is a mental one that precedes them. Liu and Noppe-Brandon express this idea this way: "The quality and durability of any creative act depend in great measure on the fertility and force of the imagination that feeds the act. This is where it all begins. We reap what we sow."[235] It involves developing a detailed picture in your mind. Jenny Blake describes this process as being more about play than willpower, asserting, "If you would like to entertain certain opportunities, put your attention on that idea or reality in your imagination first."[236] In 1905, Thomas Edison listed imagination amongst the most important qualities of an inventor, along with looking for analogies.[237] Imagination precedes invention. As William Arthur Ward famously said, "If you can imagine it, you can achieve it." Is the reverse also true, that if you can't imagine it, you can't achieve it? I suspect so.

Vision can also be defined as a product of imagination. But the two are different in a practical sense. Many organizations take time in their strategic planning cycle to articulate their corporate vision. Developing it happens once every five years or more. The vision then hangs on the wall as a statement, alongside their mission and values. Because people anticipate that use for a vision statement, they tend to spend longer wordsmithing it than they do fleshing out the details of it. They rarely develop a shared, rich picture of that vision. Moreover, vision is often framed as an ideal state, inferring that it will never actually come into being. So, if it

IMAGINATION

is imaginary more than imagined, why would we spend much time on it? While collective imagination requires us to be visionary, my dream is for it to be embedded in our ways of working together, generating multiple "visions" across various timeframes; visions that are detailed enough to motivate concrete action toward them.

Kelli Pearson defines imaginative leadership as "The ability to influence, evoke, or shape the mental models, metaphors, and cultural narratives that people (both self and others) use to make sense of the world."[238] I appreciate her emphasis on imagination as a path to sense-making. It is also a path to productivity, empathy, and problem solving. Imagination gives us access to other people's stories. It is this interplay between storytelling and storylistening that makes imaginative leadership possible and powerful.[239]

In my experience, imagination is the step that is most often neglected in innovation planning or even design thinking. For many of us, our imagination muscles are weak from underuse, both alone and in groups. There are likely many reasons for this, including our strong preference for predictability. For instance, Dr. Jason Fox suggests that our tendency to reduce uncertainty leads to a reduction in what he calls our "pioneering resources" such as imagination and serendipity, leading to incremental and opportunistic improvements.[240] An analysis of the 9/11 emergency response cited a "failure of imagination" that an attack of that nature was even possible.[241] Leaders must navigate the tension between imagination and knowledge. We need to believe something is possible before we can pursue or prevent it. According to Ben Hardy, "When people say, 'I can't imagine that,' they're usually talking about their own lack of imagination, and not about the unlikelihood of the event that they're describing."[242]

We also lack time. Oliver Burkeman asserts, "We've been granted the mental capacities to make almost infinitely ambitious plans, yet practically no time at all to put them into action."[243] I would argue that few people choose to invest their limited time in imagining infinitely ambitious plans in the first place.

IMAGINATION

In the absence of imagination, we should not be surprised that we continue to do what we have always done. Decisions based on evidence and experience alone may be credible and familiar, but they are highly unlikely to be disruptive or generative. Those decisions are based on lag indicators. Their genesis has status quo baked in. They lead us to "continuous improvement" or tinkering. In contrast, imagination leads us into new territory, where transformation becomes possible.

There is more at stake in perpetuating status quo decisions than the risk of boredom. Given the accelerating pace of change discussed in the previous chapter on adaptability, as Marshall Goldsmith is famous for saying, "What got us here won't get us there." It is increasingly unlikely that incremental tweaks today will be sufficient to stay relevant in tomorrow's marketplace. As Ross Thornley of AQai argues, "We are moving from the knowledge economy to the imagination economy."[244] Brian Paradis argues that our imaginative skills are not progressing as quickly as other societal and technological changes.[245] Without those skills, the solutions we devise risk becoming increasingly poorly suited to our rapidly evolving contexts.

Even more than that, replicating our current reality perpetuates whatever weaknesses, blind spots, and injustices characterize today's experience. We have a social responsibility to build a future that is better than the present, in more ways and for more people. A commitment to justice, equity, diversity, and inclusion compels us to engage in imaginative planning. Rob Hopkins' framing of imagination as both a responsibility and an essential skill resonates strongly with me. He cites this challenge: "If we were to be bold, brilliant and decisive, to act in proportion to the challenges we are facing and to aim for a future we actually feel good about it—what would we do?" He then quotes Neil Gaiman who writes: "We have an obligation to imagine. [...] Individuals change their world over and over, individuals make the future, and they do it by imagining things can be different."[246]

Perhaps we are already more imaginative than we give ourselves credit for. Mental models help focus our attention and guide our decision

IMAGINATION

making all the time. And they are all imagined![247, 248] We forget that we are in a continual process of making things up—beliefs and stories we live by can take on a sense of "reality" when in fact they are socially built and reinforced. As an undergraduate student in sociology, one of the core disciplinary lessons that stuck with me was the idea of social construction: that institutions and habits of behaviour are not immutable. They are created by humans and thus changeable by them. It all sounded very academic 30 years ago, but more recently it has been freshly translated in my life as, "It's all made up!" I see its relevance in relation to pricing. Three stripes of paint on a canvas could sell for $100 or $100,000 or perhaps even $100 million. That price is not directly linked to the objective quality of the product or the time spent producing it, but to what someone is willing to pay. Similarly, in certain professions, most notably in professional sports, the salaries paid are completely disproportional to the time spent or the societal impact of the activity; those price tags are linked to what people and corporations are willing to pay. It is all made up. We collectively imagine things all the time.

How to unleash it

Any graphic designer or writer of fiction facing a deadline will tell you that it is very difficult to be imaginative on demand—even more so when we are asking that of a group, as the collaborative imaginative processes are less familiar and often the stakes are higher.

You may find yourself reverting to age old narratives along the lines of, "I am just not creative" when I suggest that our imagination muscles need strengthening. But as previously explained, imagination and creativity are not synonymous anyway. Moreover, we rarely think of imagination as a skill that can be learned or strengthened. We see it as endowed, not taught. Although it is not easy to master, the first step to increasing imagination as a skill is recognizing it as learnable in the first place.

IMAGINATION

In her compelling book *Uncharted*, Margaret Heffernan suggests that imagination is particularly difficult because it surfaces conflicts and choices.[249] When we take the time to fill in the details of the sketches in our minds, we are forced to connect dreamy imagination in a fantasy world with productive imagination in the real world. That's when things get hard. Described in broad strokes, we may think we agree with someone else. Once we fill in the colour, shading, and shadows, we are more likely to discover that our mental pictures differ from others' more than we thought.

Imagination does not thrive when our basic needs are not met.[250] We are particularly resourceful, however, when resources are scarce. When things are not thriving is when we most need good ideas.[251] It is my hope that we don't need to be in deep struggle to access imagination. Perhaps our current situation, where change is outpacing our ability to adapt, will be enough to stir fresh imagination in us.

Some current trends may help us in this regard. One is the increased focus on design thinking and user experience. These methodologies are popularizing the process of collective imagining and crowdsourced creativity. Similarly, increased acceptance for the concepts of failing forward and fast, and the importance of psychological safety in teams, may help imaginative collaboration to flourish. We know that imagination is inhibited when people feel fearful, so minimizing fear in corporate settings is an important precondition to collective imagination.

As previously noted with other elements of the ELASTIC acronym, many tips for increasing imagination are generic or overlapping—stay curious, be kind, control your fear.[252] Many tips are focused on individual behaviours. They are still worth highlighting here, as imaginative people likely contribute to imaginative teams.

Some rather predictable but effective tips include seeking adventure, daydreaming, playing like a child, and taking walks.[253] A sense of wonder contributes to imagination, so stargazing or spending time in wilderness

IMAGINATION

can help. So too, perhaps unexpectedly, can surrounding yourself with a blue environment, as that colour has been found to stimulate calm creative thinking most conducive to productive imagination.

Other recommendations straddle personal and collective contexts. Do you remember I told you imagination incorporates paradox? Get ready for a few. The first is that exposure to a variety of people and contexts can also stimulate our imagination. New situations challenge our perceptions, thereby creating new neural activity. They keep us alert and attentive, even when they occur mentally through scenario planning or in real life through travel or exposure to diverse teams. Perhaps unsurprising. But here comes the kicker: new situations also create memories, and without memory we can't imagine. Neurologically, we draw from the past to imagine what lies ahead. The more we know and have experienced, the more our imaginations can produce.[254, 255, 256] At the same time, we don't want to overvalue memory. Margaret Heffernan suggests using our history to identify questions not answers. She asserts, "When we expect history to guide us, we overweight continuity and narrative, while underweighting change and contingency."[257]

Another unexpected practice for turbocharging your imagination is to provide it with edges or constraints.

> "We need the right boundaries for our imagination to elicit the choices we have. [...] People who are exceptional at framing understand that their imagination needs bounds—cognitive curbs, mental manacles—not to interdict their vision but to guide it. Restraints can free creativity rather than curtail it, providing a zone of permissibility to take mental risks."[258]

Here's another proven paradox: to be more imaginative, systematize it. In their book (with the compelling oxymoronic title), *The Imagination Machine*, Martin Reeves and Jack Fuller offer a series of steps to embed imagination in your leadership and corporate practices.[259] Like Heffernan, they recommend starting with increasing your exposure to varied and inspiring situations. They take it further by suggesting that surprise fuels imagination. So, find a way to introduce more surprise into your life! Then, rethink your mental models and build improved ones. Put effort into developing your idea. That sounds like a more familiar understanding of imaginative activity. It enters newer territory, perhaps more common in design thinking or innovation labs, with Reeves and Fuller's next suggestion to collide your idea with reality by testing and refining it inside your organization to drive its evolution. They then explore the very social and practical activity of encouraging others to adopt the idea. Over time, your novel idea becomes the new ordinary. Reeves and Fuller acknowledge the challenge of sustaining imagination during execution and highlight the importance of "keeping it kindled" as you repeat the process over and over again.[260]

We often think of imaginative inspiration as a sudden stroke of genius, but we need to give it time. Pete Davis, in his book *Dedicated*, describes the process this way:

> "By saying you are willing to work at something for a long time, you free your imagination. If we only focus on projects that we can get done quickly, what we believe to be possible is limited. But if we're willing to go slow, we can embrace grander visions, knowing that we have the time and patience to make them real."[261]

One final tip for growing imagination brings another element of the ELASTIC acronym back into play: extend trust. As adrienne maree brown encourages, don't limit others based on your lack of imagination, but instead trust people to do things better than you imagined.[262] Framing imagination as a collective activity frees us up to rely on others' brilliance to supplement and amplify our own.

IMAGINATION

CURIOSITY

The cure for boredom is curiosity.
There is no cure for curiosity.
~Dorothy Parker

What it is and why we need it

I have become curious about curiosity.

Curiosity is defined as a strong, eager desire to know or learn something. It is about being inquisitive and interested. Based on pioneering work by Berlyne, we know that curiosity can be perceptual—an increased awareness of stimuli—and epistemic—the drive to know. It generally shows up in two behavioural ways: as specific, when we take deep dives into particular pre-determined subjects, and diversive, which is a more exploratory journey of perusing possibilities.[263, 264] There is also empathic curiosity, which is a desire to understand the thoughts and feelings of others.

Curiosity can be aroused by external stimuli such as complexity, novelty, uncertainty, and conflict. If an external stimulus is too low, there will be no motivation to explore it. If a stimulus is too high, it will result in anxiety, almost paralysis. If it's just right, it will result in the desired exploratory behaviour.[265]

Tools used to measure something reveal how we define it. The transnational scientific firm Merck has produced "State of Curiosity" reports, measuring the curiosity of their workforce.[266] Merck's Multi-Dimensional, Work-Related Curiosity Scale is heavily based on the scholarship of Todd Kashdan. Kashdan's research team has identified five dimensions of curiosity as follows.

1. Joyous exploration: the desire to seek out new knowledge and information, and the subsequent joy of learning and growing.
2. Deprivation sensitivity: the tension of recognizing and seeking to reduce gaps in knowledge and the relief of a problem solved.
3. Stress tolerance: willingness to embrace the doubt, confusion, and other forms of distress that arise from exploring new, unexpected, complex, or mysterious territory.
4. Social curiosity: wanting to know what other people are thinking and doing by observing, talking, or listening to conversations overtly or covertly.
5. Thrill seeking: the willingness to take physical, social, and financial risks to acquire varied, complex, and intense experiences.[267]

Interestingly, to assess curiosity in a work context, Merck used the first three elements on Kashdan's list and replaced the final two with a fourth they called "Openness to people's ideas," which involves valuing and intentionally seeking out diverse opinions.[268, 269]

Merck found that rather than labelling someone as curious or not, it is significantly more useful to detail employees' experience of specific elements of curiosity. Kashdan's research has led to a typology of curious people:

1. The fascinated: high on all dimensions of curiosity, particularly joyous exploration.

2. Problem solvers: high on deprivation sensitivity, medium on other dimensions.
3. Empathizers: high on social curiosity, medium on other dimensions.
4. Avoiders: low on all dimensions, particularly stress tolerance.

His typology makes me curious whether these same curiosity categories could be applied to teams and organizations too.

Office supply company Viking also set out to measure curiosity, in a careful but perhaps less academically rigorous way. Their intention was to identify "the most curious country in Europe" and their measurement scale ranked these six indicators:

- Wikipedia page views per month per person with internet access.
- Active users on language-learning site Duolingo.
- Use of the internet for reading news or books.
- Number of library loans per year per capita.
- Number of Erasmus+ students per 1,000 students.[270]
- Hours spent in vocational training at work.[271]

I find it fascinating to note the inferences behind this list. Curiosity is deemed to be present if we see behaviours such as research, reading, learning a new skill, and visiting a new place. (And since I'm sure you're curious about which European country emerged as the most curious, the victor was Malta!)

Knowing things is generally highly regarded, a value which seems to transcend most cultures.[272] Merck's findings would suggest that curiosity, unlike communication, is not culturally specific. They found no significant differences in curiosity across 9,000 employees in 23 countries based on culture. They did, however find differences based on age and

CURIOSITY

stage. Curiosity was greater in new employees and those higher on the organizational hierarchy. It was highest amongst 35 to 45-year-olds and lowest in employees under 25.[273]

I am interested in Merck's age-differentiated findings, as the value attributed to curiosity has shifted generationally. For example, over 1,800 years ago, St. Augustine listed curiosity as a "temptation," driving us to discover "secrets which are beyond our understanding, which can avail us nothing and which man should not wish to learn." My great grandmother took, "Curiosity killed the cat" as common sense; she viewed asking questions as insolence, particularly of those in authority. I remember my grandmother responding to a question I had following one of her medical appointments: "If the doctor had wanted me to know that, he would have told me." The contrast with today's parenting and educational norms is striking, where inquiry-based learning is central and young people asking endless questions around the dinner table is an indicator of parental success. It leaves me wondering why the youngest generation of workers is in fact the least curious. Google might have something to do with it, as having answers instantaneously at our fingertips does not build a skill of persistent inquiry.[274]

I am also stopped short by Peter Diamandis' observation in his book *The Future Is Faster than You Think*: "Forget about the difference between generations; currently mere months can bring a revolution."[275]

These generational examples remind me that we each bring to these ELASTIC elements the stories we tell ourselves. These stories colour our interpretation of the elements in other people. For example, in our initial workshop on curiosity, we were talking about asking questions as evidence of a curious posture. A couple of us admitted that when a person doesn't ask questions in a conversation, we tend to label them as self-absorbed or disinterested. Another participant bravely reminded us that the other person may in fact be intensely curious and not narcissistic at all, but possibly very shy. As Pema Chodron advises, "Drop the storyline!"

In modern times, curiosity is almost always seen as desirable. It is highlighted as a key factor in positive intelligence.[276] As James Clear has asserted, "Being curious is better than being smart."[277] Author Adam Bryant interviewed 700 CEOs for his book *The Corner Office: Indispensable and Unexpected Lessons from CEOs on How to Lead and Succeed*. He asked them, "What qualities do you see most often in those who succeed?" Their number one answer was passionate curiosity.[278] Kidd suggests that rather than defining curiosity, it is more helpful to identify the motivations for information-seeking behaviour.[279] Let's explore a few possible reasons why curiosity is a good thing.

In interpersonal interactions, curiosity conveys presence, listening, and open-mindedness. It releases feel-good chemicals in both parties that are strongly linked to well-being. It infers a desire to build a relationship and evokes helping behaviour in others.[280] It is a strong pathway to trust. This is perhaps why being a curious leader is identified as one protective factor to reduce or prevent burnout in your workforce.[281] Curiosity is also one of the superpowers of excellent debaters, as it leads to a clearer understanding of others' perspectives. Not only does curiosity build empathy, but it conveys to the other person that you want to empathize with them.

Interestingly, although curiosity can imply wide ranging exploration, it also improves focus. In fact, it is often associated with mindfulness because of the open and attentive attitude inherent in each.[282] At the same time, it enlarges our understanding of context and nuance.

Curiosity is also a pathway to insight. Deprioritizing it can block inspiration in organizations.[283] It fuels innovation and creativity, often through not only generating but also linking ideas. Todd Henry describes this process as "meshing"—a necessary step between mapping and making, fuelled by curiosity.[284] Merck identifies curiosity as an essential skill in tackling global problems. If no one wondered how to cure a virus or reverse global warming in the first place, there would be no reason to invest in doing so. Curiosity drives motivation, experimentation and

CURIOSITY

problem solving. This idea is affirmed by Chip and Dan Heath. They argue that we need curiosity plus peripheral vision in order to see and solve problems. If we don't see them, we don't solve them.[285, 286, 287, 288] I trust you are hearing echoes with imagination here. Although curiosity follows imagination in the ELASTIC acronym, it often precedes it in real life.

Curiosity also develops patience and perseverance. It helps people learn how to learn and enjoy the learning process. Amanda Lang highlights the importance of this skill in the knowledge economy, where the winner is not the one with specific content-based expertise so much as the one who can figure out a process for solving complex problems as they arise, including in currently unfamiliar subject areas.[289] Her findings are echoed in various employability indices that identify critical thinking and problem solving as foundational skills of the future,[290] since curiosity usually lies beneath those abilities.

Lang goes on to argue that because of its strong links to positive well-being, curiosity is a path to a more energized life.[291, 292] It opens us up to wonder and is linked to greater love and vitality.[293] It activates the reward centres of the brain that light up when we learn something new or accomplish a goal. There is a strong correlation between curiosity and flourishing.[294] Curiosity adds to the longevity and quality of our lives.[295]

Curiosity helps us to manage stress, as feelings of wonder tend to reduce reactivity. A recent study confirmed, "During states of curiosity, people show a remarkable ability to tolerate potential sources of distress, being less defensive, less reactive to discomfort and difficulties, and more tolerant of uncertainty."[296, 297] Curiosity moves us forward when we are frozen or stuck. It even allows us to break bad habits more easily. James Stephens asserts, "Curiosity will conquer fear even more than bravery will." Marcus Buckingham encourages us to greet our fears with curiosity, because those fears will point us to what we love.[298]

Curiosity makes us more observant, encouraging us to think more deeply, and slowing us down before taking action. Curiosity reminds us that we do not have the full picture. This humility frequently leads us into more skillful and respectful forms of collaboration and results in a reduction in bias and less unproductive conflict.[299, 300] Curiosity reminds us that learning is fundamentally a group activity, because no one person has all the answers.

Curiosity is wise. Shirzad Chamine, ambassador of the concept of positive intelligence, identifies curiosity as a characteristic of our inner sage.[301] Dorie Clark suggests, "Curiosity builds character."[302] Curiosity is tied to emotional intelligence, social intelligence, cognitive skills, problem solving, and analytical skills.[303] It is emerging as more important than previously thought, because it helps us adapt. All successful leaders are curious.[304]

Although curiosity is almost universally seen as positive, it is also a skill that is often overlooked and underexploited. Merck and Viking are exceptions; rarely do we find companies investing explicitly in assessing or amplifying the curiosity skills of their workforce. Stephynie Malik calls it "an elite communication skill," asserting that companies should make curiosity a common core value.[305, 306] Alison Horstmeyer's research found that curiosity, when encouraged and supported within the workforce, can play a generative role in helping organizations close soft-skill gaps and better navigate ambiguity, perpetually changing business landscapes and rapidly advancing technology.[307] In *The Curious Advantage*, Ashcroft, Brown, and Jones suggest, " [A] curious organisation learns faster than a non-curious organisation. It will create and innovate faster, work better together, evolve and mutate faster in response to external shifts and build better relationships. All this leads to competitive advantage."[308]

So why does curiosity get so easily disregarded? Might this dismissive posture come from a fundamental, fixed belief that curiosity is not a learnable skill? While some argue that curiosity is a natural part of being human,[309] ask any middle school teacher and they will tell you that some

CURIOSITY

students retain their childlike curiosity while in others it fades and is hard to recapture.

Or does it come from simple hubris; there is no need to ask questions if we assume we already know the answers. As John Maxwell says, "The greatest enemy of learning is knowing."[310] Renowned basketball coach John Wooden affirms, "It's what you learn after you know it all that counts."

Or perhaps it comes from a deep-seated corporate and cultural norm that rewards those who know the answer rather than those who ask great questions. We want to look smart. We prefer to give advice than to ask for it. We favour those who know over those who ask. This brings to mind the story of a professor who was baffled by the silence in his upper year graduate seminar class. Despite the small group, interesting topic, provocative questions, and the instructor's best efforts to encourage lively dialogue, the students remained quiet. When asked about it, one participant eventually explained that no one wanted to risk looking like they didn't know the answer in front of other people. The classroom had become a place to show off what you already knew rather than to learn something new.

The irony in that story is especially powerful because curiosity should increase with knowledge. The more we know, the more we realize we don't know.[311] Adam Grant suggests that one positive ramification of imposter syndrome is that it may cause us to become more curious, as we are keenly aware of the limits of our expertise.[312] Yuval Noah Harari concurs: "Trust those who admit ignorance more than those who claim infallibility."[313]

Reluctance to embrace curiosity is not limited to the classroom. Diane Hamilton suggests that some leaders surround themselves with smart people as a substitute for their own curiosity.[314] "Leaders often think that letting employees follow their curiosity will lead to a costly mess."[315] It appears inefficient, and its return on investment is not immediately clear or measurable. Although many leaders say they welcome disruption, most would prefer to carry on unquestioned.[316] Curious inquiry frequently disrupts the status quo.

CURIOSITY

At the same time, curiosity—or at least conversations about it—seems to be on the rise. Encouragement to "get curious" is everywhere, and "I'm curious about..." is the opener for more than a few coaching conversations. It may have become code for judgement rather than true curiosity. You could substitute some variation of, "I can't believe you did/thought/ tried that crazy thing, so you'd better tell me more!" Or perhaps it has become a linguistic reminder to be more tender with ourselves and one another during a difficult season. Recent research suggests that curiosity increases with uncertainty, so perhaps its recent rise is unsurprising.[317]

This rise in popularity of assuming a curious stance rather than an expert one has been accompanied by an exponential increase in access to information, such that anyone can directly satisfy their curiosity about anything at any time. The authors of *The Power of Curiosity* predict that "Traditional knowledge bearers must adjust."[318] Democratization of access to high quality information seems like a good thing, but does it really increase curiosity? Could a rise in easily satisfied curiosity mean a loss of respect for true, hard-won wisdom?

How to improve it

I mentioned that encouragement to "get curious" is everywhere. Once you start looking for it, you'll be amazed at how frequently it comes up, and recent business and self-help writing is no exception. For instance, in her fine book *Scout Mindset*,[319] Julia Galef suggests getting curious instead of attempting to explain away our confoundment; don't write off the other side as crazy, but instead treat confusion as a clue. Similarly, adrienne maree brown says, "Get curious in your own life, about how you face change in powerful ways, in ways that show your dignity and help you stay connected to what you care about."[320]

But what if increasing our curiosity is not something we know very well how to do?

CURIOSITY

Curiosity is not necessarily something you're born with and then you lose. It is not something available in a fixed amount and some of us are allocated far more of it than others. It is not equally distributed. It is more helpful to think of curiosity as a choice to be made, a skill to be honed and a habit to be cultivated. It is a quality that can be nurtured both in individuals and in organizations.

First, model it. Ask questions, continuously learn, and admit when you don't know something. Excellent questions are at the heart of curiosity. Being open to "What if?" questions, and creating opportunities for people to share them, is integral to an inquisitive and innovative workplace.[321, 322] In his book *Questions Are the Answer,* Hal Gregersen asserts that behind every breakthrough is a better question.[323] Questioning is a learnable skill, so by getting better at questioning, you raise your chances of finding better answers.

Let me give you one example of an intentional practice of curiosity that came to me via my friend Chad Littlefield.[324] Chad's late mentor and business partner Will Wise chose to be curious, even with people who on the surface appeared not to share many interests in common with him. One day, Will came upon a man who, by all visible accounts, was a massive fan of a particular baseball team. He had the hat, the shirt, the socks, the bag... all the gear. Will was not a fan of the same team. Will did not like baseball at all. In fact, he wasn't much of a sports guy. But he did like people. So, instead of asking this man about baseball, Will asked him an even better question. He said, "Tell me how you came to be so passionate about baseball?" This carefully worded, caring inquiry catalyzed the sharing of a fascinating story about this man's relationship with his father. Both parties were rewarded for Will's curiosity, and all it took was for him to build a conversational bridge through skillful questioning. We could all learn to do the same. Imagine if leaders took seriously the task of equipping and rewarding people for asking great questions.

The potential benefits of this strategy extend far beyond our work-places. As Gary Keller affirms in *The One Thing*, how we phrase the questions we ask ourselves determines the answers that eventually become our life.[325]

> *"You can tell whether a man is clever by his answers.*
> *You can tell whether a man is wise by his questions."*
> *~Naguib Mahfouz*[326]

Second, hire for curiosity and nurture it in your team. April Rinne writes about T, Pi, and X-shaped people in her book *Flux*.[327] These are people who demonstrate a depth of knowledge in some subjects while simultaneously being broad-gauged and interested in many others.[328] As a leader, you can hire for people like that, and then create opportunities for them to continue broadening and exploring their interests. Emphasize learning goals alongside performance goals, then acknowledge people for meeting them. Perhaps the most famous example of giving employees space to explore comes from Google, where it is said that employees are given 20% of their time to dabble in creative areas of interest to them. Sadly, it is also reported that a low percentage of people actually take advantage of that unstructured time, often being overtaken by other workload demands.[329]

Third, make space. Feeling time constrained impacts our ability to be curious.[330] As with other new skills we are developing, we need to put practice time in our calendar.

And what might practising curiosity look like? Try leading with it, particularly in settings where we are tempted to tell rather than ask. Being curious, particularly in professional contexts, requires some courage (think of those students in their seminar class). Rosie Yeo affirms its benefits this way in her context: "High-performing [teams] walk in with curiosity. They are brave enough to say they don't know, and open-minded

CURIOSITY

enough to consider other perspectives and possibilities."[331] We get both better and braver with practice.

The fourth tip is to make a plan. As Ian Leslie writes in *Curious*, "We can arrange our lives to stock our curiosity or quash it."[332] Ashcroft, Brown, and Jones suggest turning your wonder into a project.[333] Chip Conley suggests being clear about how we will invest in stoking our curiosity.[334] Dorie Clark recommends that we "optimize for interesting" by seeking opportunities likely to sustain our curiosity.[335] Although these authors are targeting their advice primarily to individuals, I see no reason why it could not apply equally to teams.

Following Chip's advice, I have started to map out a curiosity plan for my next couple of years, and it's lighting me up. It involves learning (getting my coaching certification), attending events (including Chip's own Modern Elder Academy, I hope), and visiting new places (hopefully our Scandinavian tour, cancelled in 2020, will soon get put back on my calendar!). In the spirit of stretching, I am pushing myself not just to attend some of these inspiring events, but to do what would be required to speak at them (expressing a goal makes it more likely I'll achieve it!).

Another area of stretch for me, appropriate to ending this section of the book, is to consider how I might support organizations in developing similarly energizing curiosity plans at a collective level. That sounds like a fun challenge to me!

Never lose a holy curiosity.
~Einstein

...ISH

live in the realm of "good enough" much of the time. It's why knitting suits me better than quilting—it's less precise. "Good enough" is how I clean my house. I'd rather get a product out the door and improve it over time than wait until it's perfect. Roughly right. Ish.

I want to honour my colleague Lynne Cazaly's work in highlighting "ish" as a way of being. She writes about it, embodies it, and embraces it wholeheartedly in other people. She muses, "We often ish because we have to. So could we ish because we choose to?"[336]

Ish came to mind here for two reasons. First, because we all do the best we can; it's never perfect and that's okay. The ZOnE is a moving target, and I want to leave you with a commitment to be gentle on yourself when you over or undershoot it. Second, three other powerful words have been surfacing for me, which make the ELASTIC mnemonic too long but are tenacious enough to warrant mentioning in closing.

I – Inspiration.

S – Safety.

H – Hope.

Inspiration

We need inspiration and can be it. One of the mantras within Thought Leaders Business School (where I met Lynne) is: "Be inspired by the company you keep." Jim Rohn is credited with saying, "You are the average of the five people you spend the most time with," but David Barkus' research would suggest that we are influenced by a far wider circle than that.[337] Who we connect with matters. We always encouraged our kids to choose their friends very carefully for this reason. But perhaps it's even more powerful to turn the equation around: the people you spend the most time with will become more like you! In the context of ELASTIC leadership, this is not just a call, yet again, to "be a good human," but more specifically to be someone who believes that others can find their ZOnE even before they believe it. That belief, alongside your ability to model life in the ZOnE for them, is a potent motivator.

Safety

We need to feel safe to stretch. It's true in our bodies and it's also true in our work and teams. Google's now-famous Project Aristotle, designed to identify the qualities of effective teams, at first saw no discernable pattern across its data. Good teams did not all behave in the same way. Yet when they dug deeper, they determined that diverse, high performing teams did commonly have each other's back. Amy Edmondson, who coined the term psychological safety in the first place, defines it as, "A sense of confidence that a team will not embarrass, reject or punish someone for speaking up." It is developed in practical but varied ways, through "conversational turn taking" and higher than average "social sensitivity." Edmondson suggests that psychologically safe teams frame challenges more as learning problems than as execution ones.[338] Why highlight safety here? Because it's a necessary condition for stretchiness.

In my facilitation practice, I recognize how critical it is for participants to have a sense of safety. I am also not so naïve as to think that I have enough influence to create that threshold of safety in a short time as an outsider parachuting in to host a workshop or two. You will not hear me say, "This is a safe space. You can say anything you want!" I would be over-reaching to suggest that creating that level of safety lies within my control. It makes me sound oblivious to the pre-existing, often entrenched power dynamics inside organizations and society more broadly. What I can say is that I will facilitate a session in which people have equal opportunities to speak and in which respectful behaviour will be expected. We know that safety is more likely to flourish when those conditions are met. What could you do in your contexts to help yourself to feel safer and create safer environments for others?

Hope

I couldn't finish this book without mentioning hope. It may sound like a Pollyanna way to end, but I raise it for evidence-based reasons. Based on the work of AQai, hope is the most powerful predictor of adaptability in individuals and teams. Read that again. Of the multiple factors that comprise one's Adaptability Quotient, hope is the strongest.

Hope is more than unfounded optimism. C.R. Snyder's pioneering work in hope theory, within the field of positive psychology, defines hope as having three components: positive goals for the future, the perceived capability to derive pathways toward them, and the agency to move along those pathways.[339] As Ben Hardy explains in *Be Your Future Self Now*, without hope, motivation is impossible.[340] I look forward to continued research on how to strengthen each of these elements, as I am confident that hope, like other elements of adaptability, is a learnable skill.

...ish.

PART FOUR

The Case Studies

When I read business related books, I frequently skip the case studies. And yet here I am including them in my own book. Why is that? One main reason is that every business book I was reading (and I read a lot of them for my book club, *Wiser by Choice*) was highlighting the same few global brands. I am frankly quite tired of reading examples pulled from the largest corporations on the planet and quirky start-ups heavily funded by venture capital firms. Something gets very much lost in translation into most people's experience, and translation is always necessary when working with case studies. I am not convinced that the experiences of GE, Facebook, Pixar, and Apple are the best learning examples for most people.

I am also including case studies here because I want to honour and elevate the work of those I consider to be ordinary (but impressive!) people doing extraordinary things. We can learn about ELASTIC leadership not just from large corporate America but also from the active, innovative, and dynamic social sector in Canada. And that is where the focus of these case studies lies. These are real-life examples in recent times. They may not make headlines, but they have inspired me. As I embark on my 25th year in business, I want to recognize the work of committed creative individuals who are doing amazing things, perhaps with fewer zeroes at the end. But not always. Nonprofit does not mean small. The significance of the nonprofit sector does not only come from the gravitas of their organizational missions, but many are working at considerable scale. So, although these are not stories drawn from Amazon or Google or Warren Buffett or Sheryl Sandberg, I hope that you will find that they are more accessible as a result, and that your necessary translation of them to your own experience happens at a shorter distance than if I had focused only on Silicon Valley.

Once again, this is an arbitrary list. And a personal one, given that I limited it to people with whose work I am directly familiar. It is also quite a local one, which is perhaps surprising given that my work takes me all over the world. It has reminded me that when you lean in and examine something more closely—in your garden or beside the sidewalk—you often find it teeming with life.

ENERGY

Jim Moss and Dave Whiteside

Jim Moss and Dave Whiteside are long-time colleagues, first at Plasticity Labs and now at YMCA of Three Rivers where they lead YMCA WorkWell (https://www.ymcaworkwell.com/) with a mandate to build healthier, thriving organizations. Jim Moss is the Leader of Community Development at YMCA WorkWell, the former founder/CEO/Chief Happiness Officer at Plasticity, and a former professional lacrosse player. Dr. Dave Whiteside is the Director of Insights at YMCA WorkWell and YMCA of Three Rivers and the former Director of Research and Insights at Plasticity. Dave and Jim are collaborators rather than clients of mine. I regularly use their research in my work as it offers relevant, rigorous, accessible and recent Canadian evidence.

Energy and elasticity

"I love the metaphor of elastics because, like us, an elastic can stretch and then, if it's healthy, come back to its natural shape," says Jim. "At the same time, an elastic just sitting on the counter has no purpose. An elastic needs to be engaged to be useful."

Jim Moss
Photographer: Hilary Gauld

Dave Whiteside
Photographer: Hilary Gauld

"We are at our best when we're not comfortable but not too uncomfortable, either" says Dave. "You want your elastic band to be stretched just enough."

For Jim, who sees energy as a kind of currency, a big question is: "Am I expending realistic energy in terms of efficiency so that there's forward action on goals? How am I feeling at the end of the week—am I tired but looking forward to next week? Or am I sapped and not sure I want to do that again or not feeling like it was worth it?" In other words: is my elastic stretched too far or not enough?

Jim reflects on YMCA WorkWell's observations about how organizations can help their people find the right amount of stretch. "In the work we do, we learn about how culture should provide an efficient structure for us to accomplish shared goals, giving us a good return on our energy investment. When culture is weak or inefficient, everyone has to work harder than they should to accomplish goals. If that continues, people burn out, spending more energy than they should."

Depletion and burnout

"Today, there's a very interesting macro-trend we've observed in the data and with our partners that I've never witnessed in the past," says Dave. "Currently we're seeing two groups of almost equal sizes in organizations. One group is incredibly burned out, has no energy at all, and wants to have everything taken off their plates. The other half are people who are incredibly energized and raring to go. There are few people in the middle."

The challenge of this split, Dave says, is, "Those who are burned out do not have the energy to match the energized group, and those with energy feel like they have to pull the others along." Jim adds that the two groups can cause stress for each other, and that people are still adjusting to this situation of imbalance. He also observes, "When you have clear role definitions on a team, you know how to play well together and you have a high level of trust that your teammates will do their job. If I start worrying about how you're doing your job, it's a distraction from me doing mine."

There is also concern about those who are depleted. Dave says when people are depleted and lacking energy, often they aren't aware of how burned out they actually are. "We often talk about a 'breakdown,' which makes it sound like one distinct moment but in reality, it's often been a more progressive trend that they just didn't have the self-awareness to see in time."

How to recharge

"A rope has no elasticity at all. A fan belt is minimally elastic but when it breaks it's catastrophic. Some polymers are almost endlessly elastic." says Jim. "There are different kinds of elastics. Some people do great in a crisis because they thrive in that. Others do it if they have to but it's more costly." He notes we become more adaptive the more we focus on what we're good at.

Dave adds an important caveat. "It's important to make sure you're elastic in work you really enjoy. You want to be stretched in work that matters to you, and that gives you more stretch."

Sometimes, Jim observes, we have to "take a knee" before being able to come back healthier and excited about the work we do.

There's also a role for organizations, Dave says: "We can tackle exhaustion that comes from cynicism and a sense of ineffectiveness by tapping into meaning. That energizes people. If people have a crystal-clear sense of priorities so they can do what matters most for them and their organization, that can be a really valuable source of energy."

Jim adds that organizations can recharge their organizational energy in a variety of ways: a fast one is to bring in new talent, although this can result in dissonance on teams. He says, "Recharging after burnout is a slow process that takes time, so ideally you want people to be recharging before they burn out."

Dave also observes that, "COVID has been a kind of natural experiment that's allowed us to know where we could stretch and where it's not optimal." Jim says, "Some have a growth mindset where they say, 'Don't waste a crisis,' while others still want to retreat to safety." The stretch has also changed people; Jim says, "I'm differently useful now. We might wish we were the elastic we were before, but we can do more if we embrace the elastic we are now."

Managing energy

Jim observes that managers have been trained to manage in person and have strong data collection and analysis skills for in-person leadership. "There are more blind spots in managing remotely and we don't yet have explicit tools to get the missing data because a lot of it was subconscious or instinctual."

That doesn't mean managing remote or hybrid staff doesn't work. Jim says, "It's not because it can't work, but because leaders aren't doing what they need to make it work." Dave returns to the metaphor of elasticity, saying, "Some leaders aren't stretching enough, and their personal elasticity is limiting the success of their group. They might half-heartedly embrace hybrid work, for example, while believing it won't work, and it becomes a self-fulfilling prophecy."

But, Dave cautions, "This will expand the haves and the have nots. Those leaders and organizations doing hybrid for the right reasons and using the right tools and putting money behind it will end up with the top talent while those who are stuck in the old ways will be left with the leftovers."

Emma Rogers

Emma is the CEO of the Children's Foundation of Guelph and Wellington. She is also the co-founder of Guelph Gives, a community charitable initiative to encourage civic philanthropy and business engagement. She formerly worked in private sector wealth management but migrated back to invest her strong leadership skills in the community sector. I have admired Emma's energy and community commitment for many years and am pleased to be working with her on a new strategic plan.

Energy as currency: how do you get some?

"Energy has always been a form of currency, but the past few years have really taught us the importance of it," says Emma. "It's the most valuable thing I can give someone, and vice versa."

Emma says of herself, "I think of myself as adaptable and I thrive on innovation and new ideas. That energizes me. It's also what drew me to the sector. I'm energized because I love what I do. My work fuels me and gives passion and purpose to what I do and how I do it."

She also believes that "Energy is contagious. There's that old saying that people won't remember what you said or did, but they will remember how you made them feel. That's energy. It's what makes people willing to follow you into the unknown."

At the same time, Emma says, it's important for a leader to acknowledge when their own energy is depleted, and to be vulnerable enough to express that to their team and even their board. She says that, paradoxically, this is energizing to a team because it models authenticity so they can bring their true selves to the table, rather than spending energy trying to pretend to be thriving. It is true positivity and encouragement that makes people want to be part of such a team.

Emma Rogers
Photographer: Hilary Gauld

"What energizes our team the most, though, is hearing individual stories of the children and youth who are impacted by our programs," says Emma. "There's a lot of demand and important needs in our sector but when we hear about a child with a full tummy or a youth with their first pair of shoes that no one else has worn before, that shows us our energy has been well-invested and it energizes us to keep going."

Elasticity helps impact

A conversation about energy quickly turns to one about burnout and compassion fatigue. "The majority of people in our sector, whether they are on the frontlines or not, are inundated with work right now. Our work got flipped at the start of the pandemic and we were all working far longer hours than we had before. I'm seeing significant burnout and compassion fatigue." Additionally, Emma says, there are unexpected human demands: donor calls that might typically last five minutes are now taking an hour, sometimes because this is the first phone call a lonely donor has had in a month.

Further adding to this, Emma says, is the reality that the social good sector is devoted to making every dollar have a direct impact. "We tend to forget that those programs depend on our staff. I am a strong advocate for our staff and everyone in our sector to care for themselves. It's a misunderstanding of the social good sector to focus solely on programs. I believe we need a change in mindset to say that it is a solid investment to care for team members and to allow them to care for themselves. If they are able to come to work as their best selves, they will be better at their jobs and then downstream a child will get a nutritious lunch and be able to participate and thrive at school and eventually go on to break the cycle of poverty and be a strong contributing member of community. This really starts with investing in a strong team and hiring enough staff."

"It's not just 'feel good' and 'you should volunteer.' We have a whole sector burning out because of limited and worn-out staff. To borrow the elasticity metaphor, at some point that elastic will snap."

Emma works at leading by example—"Gone are the days of idolizing the workaholic on their laptop till midnight"—but is also developing a strong infrastructure and culture at her organization to support this. This includes a benefits program, counselling support, wellness days, and a culture club that plans fun team activities. These efforts are not pep rallies, Emma says, but strategic and compassionate ways to reduce burnout and increase engagement and retention. Her organization also has honest conversations with all staff and especially those experiencing burnout to find out what they need to be able to show up well at work. She also advocates for paying attention to the rhythms of work. "For us, December is a busy period, but January is slower, so we take time in January to reenergize."

Energy is a team sport

When Emma describes her team as incredible and explains how they work together, the word synergy comes to mind. "We have a culture where people are comfortable sharing ideas, and no idea is a bad one. We have regular check ins that help us know what team members are going through, and because we have strong communication and respect, the team knows we have each other's backs."

Emma is clear that the energy that comes from a team isn't a question of extroversion or high physical energy, but rather a willingness to support one another, enjoy successes together, and to come up with ideas collaboratively.

Her favourite recent example of this occurred in March 2020. Before this, the organization had supported children in camps and school feeding programs, but when all of these closed along with schools, they had to alter their programming quickly. "As soon as our team knew kids were at home and didn't have access to activities or food, without hesitation they began thinking outside the box, asking: what can we do to support these kids?" The team quickly switched their model to developing activity kits locally and found ways of getting food to local families. "It energized our community to see us think of creative solutions to support children and the economy—they said it gave them a sense of purpose at a time when we were all consumed with fear and anxiety."

Emma believes this speaks highly to the character of the people on her team, noting that many skills can be taught as long as staff come to work with a growth mindset and a willingness to do whatever it takes.

Mission directs energy

Energetic people can do whatever it takes... but they don't simply do whatever. Emma says, "Staying within your mission and vision is best for the organization but it also protects that energy. Have the power to say no and give an opportunity to someone else whose vision better aligns with the opportunity. That's how a strategic plan is good for everyone within the organization. Strategic planning also allows us to look back at what worked and what didn't work so that we don't try to simply go back to what was or keep doing what we've been doing but instead we bounce ahead."

LIKEABILITY

John Neufeld

John has been the Executive Director of House of Friendship since 2009 and has received multiple awards for his community leadership. I tease John that he is one of my favourite people to work with, because he is! We have collaborated on two strategic plans and multiple other coaching and planning assignments related to addressing the social determinants of health.

Knowing yourself and your people

"The challenge of leadership is to stretch ourselves and others to the right amount of tension," says John. "If we don't invite people to stretch enough, we don't tap into their gifts and strengths, but if they stretch too far, we end up dealing with burnout and other challenges." As John thinks about the last few years, he takes the metaphor of elasticity into the realm of stretching before a race. "You always hope you've done your preparation and stretches so that when you're suddenly forced to run a marathon, you're ready."

For John, a key aspect of that preparation comes down to investing in relationships. When he reflects on the challenges of the last few years, he says, "If you didn't invest in relationships and a strong culture that

LIKEABILITY

John Neufeld
Photographer: Hilary Gauld

provided support, you couldn't go as far." For John, this means connecting genuinely at a human level, remembering someone's child's name, caring about people as human beings with full lives.

It also involves knowing the strengths of your team. "We work hard at knowing each other's strengths and tapping into those." John's team at House of Friendship uses the Strengthsfinder system to give language to particular abilities, and then they play to those strengths, encouraging people to do what they are best at. Not surprisingly, John's own strengths have been identified as building relationships and connecting with people.

This investment in knowing and respecting one another's strengths also allows John and his team to recognize where those strengths can become liabilities. "I know I lean toward stretching too far and that our team is packed with people who are achievers. Our strategic and annual plans are always too ambitious and we often have to do a reality check halfway through the year to figure out what we need to say no to."

Add value

As John reflects on likeability, he says, "True likeability is not about being popular. There's a difference between a class clown and an influential leader." John says, "You may be a dynamic, innovative person who is fun to be around, and we know from social science research that people are more willing to partner with someone who is likeable in these ways. But we also know that what people most look for in a leader is whether they do what they say. If you can't be relied upon, it takes a hit on your leadership and your likeability. The difference between a strong leader and the class clown is that the leader works hard and delivers on promises."

Being likeable is not an end in itself to John. "I often get asked about how to become an executive director, but I don't think that's the right way to think about it. It's not about how to try to become liked and to get the position." Instead, John says, "One of the best pieces of advice I was ever given was to look for ways to add value to other people's lives. When

you focus on how to help others, opportunities will naturally come up."
For John this means introducing people to one another, sharing books
you think someone else would appreciate, trying to understand others'
worlds, and being curious about their lives and how to help them. "You
might be sending out a newsletter to market your business, but you look
for ways to offer value to the lives of those reading it. People recognize this
quality and are attracted to it and follow you in a more meaningful way."

Shadow side to superpowers

Another intentional practice John sees in likeable leaders is, "They are
constantly doing their inner work and share that vulnerably. They don't
always present themselves as having it all together."

Here, John practices what he preaches. "Being liked is important to me
because of my personal story. I am an immigrant and I didn't have a great
experience coming to Canada because I just didn't fit in. That's why I'm
passionate about House of Friendship—because we make sure everyone
belongs." But that passion has a dark side to it too. "As a leader, you have
to make tough decisions that don't make you likeable. That isn't hard for
some leaders but for me, it took a long time and a lot of inner work to
recognize my triggers about wanting to be liked. People say everyone
likes me and that I'm so likeable, but the shadow side of this is developing
the willingness to make gutsy decisions." Now that this awareness is conscious for John, he says, "It doesn't get in the way as much because I can
quickly run it through my head. Now I tell people that sometimes you will
make decisions that will make you unlikeable, and that's part of being a
good leader."

Courage and passion

John says, "I've learned a lot over time about maintaining relationships
while doing something that's unpopular." For John this comes down to
having deep confidence in a decision. He recalls the time he made an

unpopular decision to close several programs for women, children, and youth. "We had done the groundwork and I knew in my heart of hearts that it was the right thing to do." But because relationships are important to John, he says, "I thought through who the decision would impact, who wouldn't be happy about it, and I took the time to communicate the decision to them and then gave them space." In this instance, some of the unhappy constituents later said that they could see this was the right decision.

"It takes courage to make such decisions at the time, though," he admits. "You surround yourself with wise people, gather good counsel, listen a lot and gather enough information to act, but you will never have perfect or enough data. As a leader, you will have to make a call and act."

For John it comes down to believing in what you're doing. He reflects on a recent purchase and renovation of a hotel that is establishing a new model for shelter. "It's been a major risk and there have been a lot of challenges and difficult decisions. In dark moments when I thought it would all fall through, I've had to believe in this so that when I do communicate about it, people understand there is a conviction there. At some level when you're passionate about what you do because you know it matters, you are likeable even to those who don't agree with you."

LIKEABILITY

Annette Aquin and Terry Cooke

Annette and Terry are close collaborators and colleagues at Hamilton Community Foundation where Annette has served as Executive Vice President Finance and Operations since 2012 and for eight years before that was VP Finance and Administration, coming in as a consultant from the private sector. Terry has been the President and CEO at the foundation since 2010. Before that, he was the president of a management consulting firm, a for-profit group of businesses and a regional municipality.

The trouble with likeable

Terry begins our conversation about likeability by talking about key friendships and saying, "I am a collector of good friends over long periods of time," but Annette is quick to point out that being well-liked and having likeability as your goal are two very different things: "Likeability in itself should not be a goal. Instead, it could be an outcome of the work you do— and how you do it."

They observe that as community foundation leaders, they are engaged in issues that can be more divisive than those faced by many other organizations, whether that is a casino in the community or the decision to build light-rail transit. "People don't always agree with us or the stance we've taken" Annette says.

The stances they take as an organization are rooted firmly in research and the organization's values. "We can work within our values and still be flexible" Annette says. "We always ask: is this moving our mission forward or is it just something someone thinks we should do?" Within our values, decisions are evidence-based, informed opinions. For Annette, it comes down to authenticity but also the ability to wrap strategy and day-to-day operations around mission.

For Terry, it's a matter of trust. Terry observes that "Trust comes from bringing the bad news first. One of my mantras with our board is that there's no challenge we can't overcome, but if we don't put difficult stuff on table, we won't build trust and momentum." The same is true in building relationships with the community. Annette says, "It's like being in any relationship: acting in a way that tries to get someone to like you rarely works out. We lead with our mission, vision, and values and invite donors to join us."

Exercising elasticity

At the same time as the foundation focuses on strategy driven by their mission, Annette says they are also opportunistic. "Community changes and we don't want to serve our strategic plan while failing to serve our community. One of our strengths is spending a lot of time looking out and responding."

The organization's pandemic response fund is an example of this elasticity. When the pandemic struck, Annette says, "We took a deep breath and changed directions, deciding to focus on what we could do as rapidly as possible." Within six weeks, they had proactively directed a significant amount of granting into the hands of organizations working on the front lines.

But this elasticity predated COVID 19. It began several years before with a Foundation board that recognized that while events happen in the community very quickly, the board itself meets several times a year. They established a Strategic Opportunities Fund and gave staff the authority to act promptly in cases of time-sensitive need. When the pandemic hit, this preparation allowed the organization to be far more nimble in responding to the needs of their partners.

Terry observes, "Too often, people make leadership and management more complex than it needs to be. We start by trying to understand those we work with and, where we can, we work with those who share

Annette Aquin
Photographer: Hilary Gauld

Terry Cooke
Photographer: Hilary Gauld

our values, passions, and deep commitment to leaving the place better than we found it." He acknowledges that there is complexity in running an organization well and that leaders need to pay attention to key metrics, but at the core it comes back to certain first principles: "Treat people with respect, give people autonomy to do work under a shared understanding, commit to being part of something bigger than yourself."

For all organizations, the pandemic showed what was in place and where there were cracks. Annette says, "We saw that the fund had prepared us as a board and staff to be change-ready."

Past and future

Being prepared was not a matter of good luck. As Terry says, "When you run a foundation, you are mindful of the shoulders you stand on and that the work you do today will only manifest itself after you're gone. We think about the long game because we are here forever and, as such, we can do things governments and other shorter-term groups can't or won't do." Annette also acknowledges the debt to those who have donated in the past. "We are beneficiaries of previous donors' legacies, often through donations from people's estates."

As both Annette and Terry approach retirement from their current roles within the next few years, they are thinking about their own legacies and succession planning, and how they can pass relational batons well to the next generation.

This begins with hiring well, Terry says, adding, "Values trump skills every time." It also involves ensuring "the things we had the benefit of—a chance to experiment and fail, autonomy in making decisions, truly being part of the team—are available" to those they hire. Annette mentions the value of mentoring the next generation of leaders by talking about the whys and hows of organizational history, bringing staff to board meetings, introducing them to donors, community, and provincial and national partners while learning from their experiences and networks.

Both note, "It's not as if we bequeath relationships to the next generation. Most people who want to work for us are people who by nature are community-minded so they have their own networks." Terry adds, "Part of leaving a good legacy is managing your own ego so that you can create space for the next person to do what is best."

"Board succession is always the number one priority," Annette says. "There's nothing more important than a strong board that knows how to govern, is committed to vision and is courageous."

Collaboration and power

Not only do Terry and Annette acknowledge a debt to those who came before them, but also those who stand beside them.

Annette says, "Collaboration has been one of our core values for a long time. We are clear that silos are a death knell to community change. We always try to involve a range of partners and we sit on boards of national organizations who are trying to make change. We aren't in a position to exclude anyone or be competitive."

Both Terry and Annette credit their board of directors for living out this value, particularly in terms of allowing them to lead in the Canadian foundation space nationally, and in listening to one of their major donors who advised them to put their assets into action through impact investment to earn a financial return with a positive social or environmental outcome.

They also acknowledge the power imbalance they hold as a funder, and work hard at being equitable and inclusive. "We are striving harder and harder to address our blind spots and deficits, whether that is EDI across the organization, or reducing barriers to entry so that everyone truly has access to our funds," Annette says, adding, "Likeability is an outcome, but not a goal in itself."

LIKEABILITY

ADAPTABILITY

Hayley Kellett and Jay Reid

Hayley and Jay are the co-founders of The Making-Box. Initially launched in 2013 as an improv school and comedy theatre, the company has evolved to become a training organization that builds adaptability in leaders around the world. They have partnered with companies you've likely heard of, such as Shopify, Google, RBC, and hundreds more. Before The Making-Box, Hayley taught and performed with The Second City, while Jay studied marketing and entrepreneurship, and worked as a trainer for the Canadian Improv Games. I've been honoured to coach and learn from Hayley and Jay. We are collaborators within the emerging global network of AQ professionally certified coaches.

Letting go

The Making-Box, as one of their employees likes to say, "is an experiment that's gone terribly right." But it certainly is an ongoing experiment and case study in adaptability, having shifted its model and way of delivering its services almost constantly.

That it has thrived while doing so is largely due to leaning into their history in theatrical improvisation, and it is these same improvisational skills and principles that they offer to their clients.

Jay Reid and Hayley Kellett
Photographer: Hilary Gauld

When Hayley moved to Guelph and was introduced to Jay, she realized they shared a passion for improv and an appreciation for what it can do in people's lives on- and off-stage. They quickly joined forces to offer comedy shows and improv classes. This led to them launching Canada's most successful theatre Kickstarter to build a storefront theatre and training centre in Guelph. They also developed an arm of their business that uses improv to develop teams at work and in the classroom. "[When the pandemic began,] we moved our experiments online," Jay says, but admits he wasn't sure the work would translate well. But translate it did, and Jay and Hayley quickly realized that what had at first looked like a problem was an opportunity; they were now able to work with individuals and teams around the globe.

ADAPTABILITY

This success also forced them to clarify their priorities in order to make some big fundamental decisions about how they would operate. Would they shift online? Close their training centre permanently? Temporarily? "Any change is arbitrary if we don't know what we want to accomplish," Jay says. "In the first lockdown when we closed, we sat down to get clear on our purpose. We agreed we would have the greatest impact if we focused on teams and organizations." More recently, their work has shifted back to more in-person work and, as Hayley says, "will probably shift again. But I'm open and excited about the possibility of connecting in ways I can't predict."

This goes right back to the principles of improv that Jay and Hayley draw upon in their work. Hayley says, "Improv skills help us live in uncertainty with joy—not knowing what will happen but knowing it will be okay." They draw on and teach four improv principles in their work to allow change to be energizing rather than depleting. The first of these is perhaps the most challenging: letting go.

Both Jay and Hayley acknowledge that letting go is challenging for most of us because there is grief in letting go. "I had to let 90% of my original role go," Hayley says. "I've taken my skills and knowledge and readjusted them so that I am excited about diving into our work with business teams, but letting go was still hard."

The improvisation practices Hayley and Jay have engaged in for years equipped them to adapt when they were grieving, so they have confidence in bringing the same skills to corporate teams to equip them for their own letting go. They describe a recent workshop where they helped a workplace team practise the discomfort of newness through an activity that exposed them to uncertainty and gave them an opportunity to acknowledge their resulting feelings.

Noticing more

The second improv principle is that of noticing more. Jay and Hayley pay attention to how they can authentically support their clients; "People are often told to be adaptable without being told what good adaptability looks like," Jay says. "They can wonder whether it's just code for 'get with the program.'"

Sometimes it is. Jay and Hayley have noticed a kind of faux adaptability in situations where leaders focus on individual solutions rather than addressing systemic problems. "It's easier to overfocus on an individual and to ignore the ways in which policies and other systemic issues are really at the heart of the problem."

This is also why The Making-Box began using the Adaptability Quotient. Just as they began their own organizational shifts by focusing on their purpose, they say, "None of us can improve our adaptability unless we know and measure where we're at."

Using "yes, and" philosophy

The third (and best-known) improv principle is the philosophy of "yes, and." When an improviser says or does something, even if it looks like a disaster or a mistake, the next person continues and builds on it. Hayley likens this to the Japanese art form of kintsugi where a broken pottery bowl is mended and even increased in value by being repaired with gold.

They describe how this principle helps polarized teams. Hayley says, "We expect a difference of opinions on teams; the 'yes, and' principle reminds people that saying yes does not mean agreement but allows them to delay evaluation and accept the other person rather than blocking or denying them. 'Yes, and' helps us work together in polarized situations."

Finding the fun

The final and core improvisational principle that encourages adaptability is, Hayley says, "Embracing playfulness in everything we do."

They both have confidence in this principle, pointing to studies that demonstrate the practical value of humour in work and the essential quality of psychological safety for building teams, safety that is practised in improv exercises. At the same time, they acknowledge the unease of some clients in engaging in improvisation. To address this, they build psychological safety by setting up expectations and operating principles, and stripping away myths and misconceptions so that no one has to fear they are being required to do something too vulnerable. "You may think you haven't done improv before," Jay says, "but any conversation with another person requires improvisation."

"There are deeper outcomes in the notion of practising playfulness together," he continues. "For instance, research shows that if we start a gathering with a five-minute improvisation activity, you will get more participation and focus in the content that follows... coming together as a team in a practice that is united and playful helps you rise to a task differently."

Catherine Wassmansdorf

Catherine Wassmansdorf is the Education Program Manager at The Riverwood Conservancy in Mississauga, Ontario. She manages student and therapeutic horticulture education programs and has personally delivered outdoor education instruction to more than 12,000 high school students. Catherine has been a coaching client of mine and is a long-time friend. I appreciate her ongoing efforts to learn new skills and gentle persistence to affect organizational change.

Finding the keys to personal adaptability

It can be easy to forget the paralyzing early days of 2020 lockdown, but while many people went from using a computer at work to using a computer at home and others didn't have the luxury of working remotely, for Catherine, the move online meant an absolute reinvention of her work. In her usual work at The Riverwood Conservancy, Catherine and her team of educators are outside every day on trails with classes of children and youth, sparking interest in the natural environment and making connections with school curricula.

"Working from a bedroom office instead of a forest ravine by the Credit River, and at a time when no one could be anywhere other than their yard, was a time of significant uncertainty and exhaustion," Catherine says. No longer could she read body language to know whether she would need to adapt her programming. She also says, "Before, my own energy in a group could be '*Wow! Look at this amazing thing!*' and people would come and look and decide whether it was exciting. In digital space, you lose all that human interaction."

Adapting her work had to begin with finding ways to adapt personally. She started with techniques she already had. "After an hour-long online

ADAPTABILITY

Catherine Wassmansdorf
Photographer: Hilary Gauld

meeting, I would go for a walk. I would work on a computer for a few hours and then I would go outside to replenish." She also began an experiment in using binoculars and a microscope to be able to see the world differently even when she was restricted to a limited space. "Changing my depth of view was a way I found to bring that sense of exploration in my mind—it gave me new sparks for learning and energy."

What helps you adapt?

Adapting was not simply a matter of personal practice.

One key to adapting came through support from Catherine's organization leader. "Our executive director said, 'Take your time. You'll get there. I believe in you.' That confidence at a time of so many other uncertainties couldn't have been more helpful. It gave us some breathing room."

It also helped to be anchored in the shared mission of their organization. "The people I work with are all mission-driven, believing in the importance of protecting our ecosystems, and that the best way of doing that is to help people find a sense of awe." Despite changing circumstances, Catherine says she and her colleagues held on to the core of their *why*.

They also backed each other up so that resilience was built into their small team. The educators learned more about each other's work so that they could pivot across their team as needed.

As Catherine began developing digital programs, her own children were able to help her with both technical and moral support. "I also turned to professional coaching with Rebecca to think through some strategies for my work. Coaching is time and resources well spent. We see medical specialists for particular concerns, and we can do the same with strategic coaching."

One of the things that best helped Catherine adapt, she says, was when students engaged on live videos. She also says she was inspired

ADAPTABILITY

to adapt her work due to the grief she felt for the teens she worked with whose lives had suddenly contracted.

Adapting the program

Catherine began designing an interactive digital visit to Riverwood, recreating an onsite retreat for people living in urban apartments without access to the natural world. It was well-received, and Catherine says, "It was the first time that I thought I might have something to contribute through web-based instruction."

She and her colleagues began learning what translated well online. What became most popular were visits with the Centre's classroom pets. "I think it was because it was unscripted and real, and it allowed students to respond and react. We began offering a Turtle Time program with our elementary, high school, and special needs clients." They also began to learn that the digital space had some advantages: "We can change time a little because we can rewind and watch something again." One of Catherine's colleagues developed engaging programming for medically fragile clients with special needs, something that can be used again during winter months or flu season.

They had to pivot again and again as classes began to haltingly return to in-person teaching. At first, programs could only take place outside and without access to on-site facilities, and therefore had to be adapted to use limited tools. When classes were able to come on-site and indoors, the organization recognized this required direction from their executive director as well as new conversations about organizational safety and duty of care.

"We now have a new capacity due to our digital programs—if a teacher is sick or there's inclement weather, we don't have to cancel but can shift online," Catherine says. "And if a class is really passionate after a visit, we can follow that up with a virtual classroom visit. We have a sense that we

ADAPTABILITY

have forged multiple pathways that will help us if and when we have to adapt again."

Limits to adaptability (and how to adapt to those limits)

Not all outdoor instructional programs translated well to an online format, Catherine says. Some simply made students feel like they were missing out, while in other cases it was impossible to capture something clearly enough. Catherine says they were also conscious of vast free online resources produced by large, well-equipped organizations. She notes that their program delivery team hadn't had to evaluate their work so directly based on market value before, but as school-based revenue dried up for nearly two years and as some funders shifted their donations to other priorities, this became a pressing concern.

Catherine reached a personal limit with adapting, too, saying that eventually the constant stress of continually stretching and trying to learn new ways of doing took a toll on her physical and mental health. "I always used to 'keep on keeping on,'" she says. "My new pivot is figuring out how to keep the lessons from all I've learned during the pandemic and look after myself at the same time."

In this pivot she has learned to ask for help, even with small questions. "I've discovered that people are happy to be asked, and there's joy in passing on what you've learned." She also says, "If you're in a work environment where you have supportive collegial relationships, it's a great use of time to maintain them. It isn't always convenient, but during challenging times of transition, collegial support builds in the resilience you need." Catherine has also become supportive of the concept of working slightly under capacity so people can have a reserve of energy for shifts that require quick adaptation.

STRATEGY

Devon Page

Devon is a lawyer and the outgoing Executive Director of Ecojustice, a role he held from 2009 to 2022. He is also an avid cyclist and runner. I supported Devon as he led the development of Ecojustice's most recent strategic plan, and I appreciate my ongoing relationship with his team as they implement the integrated program strategy that emerged from it.

We're better than we used to be

When Devon considers the ways in which his work is elastic, he begins with how his organization operates because, "I suspect people working in the environmental community would be at the high end of the scale of those who are taxed by their work. For us, being mission-aligned means devoting every day to protecting the planet, so that's a challenge when we're not at our best." He adds, "It's really clear to me that COVID has changed us, and we're still figuring out an appropriate management response."

Before COVID, he says, staff surveys showed a high degree of engagement, mission alignment, and morale. During COVID, however, like many organizations, Ecojustice moved to a remote work model and changed

Devon Page
Photographer: Grace Robertson

the way their staff related. "I really understand the metaphor of an elastic," he says. "It stretched us."

But now, Devon says, "We've largely come back and we're grappling with the fact that our elastic is slightly loose." A lot of this has to do with hybrid work. "The question we're asking is whether we can be as effective in a hybrid and remote environment now that we know what that's like."

The organization, he says, is approaching this as an opportunity. "We've always had the belief that we should hire the best people wherever we find them. Now, in enabling remote work, we can actually do that." This offers a big advantage to staff who no longer have to live in or commute to downtown Vancouver with its high housing prices.

Devon also wonders whether the question of effectiveness—*are we as good as we used to be?*—is, in fact, the wrong question to ask. Instead, he says, "We've all been handed trauma as an organization over the last few years—and we've survived. Why aren't we thinking about the ways we are better and stronger than we were before?" He clarifies this to recognize that many individuals have very challenging situations, but adds, "As an organization, we aren't terrified any more. Our donors are increasing their support. We could be saying: 'Having been tested, we're up to more. If we handled that, we can handle anything.'"

STRATEGY

Where strategy goes right... and wrong

For Devon, strategy is simply a question of operationalizing vision. This means starting with a vision and then figuring out how it guides the day-to-day tasks of an organization. "I think of it like a map with a Point A and a Point B and the strategy is the path to get there."

There are a few places he's seen this go wrong, however. "If I think of the strategic plan processes that fail, they are most often at risk in the translation from strategy to operation. I think this is simply because doing this is hard and too often other things get in the way. People often think that the goals are the end of the process, but that's maybe only ten percent of the process. Strategy isn't finished until you know how it guides your day-to-day work."

He also observes, "Different people have different aptitudes, abilities, and appetites for this kind of conversation." He notes that some people can talk about the future but struggle to identify discrete steps, while others love coming up with a plan but wait for the vision to be developed. "Ideally you have a leadership team that combines those attributes. Good leaders have to encompass both the ability to envision a future state and have an aptitude, or at least a sense of appreciation, for how to get there." In his own organization, about half the staff, including Devon, are lawyers. He recognizes that lawyers are often better at seeing the trees—the details and implications—and struggle to see the forest, or the big picture.

Another challenge is particular to nonprofits and charities, he says, where too often an organization will only roughly identify their goals before focusing on what funders will fund. His organization historically built their plans based on funder appetite, but not long after Devon took on the executive director role, he and the philanthropy director, with the support of the board, made a huge decision about funding. "The work leads," Devon says. "Our number one rule is that we don't let donors dictate strategic choices." At first, Devon says, "It was painful and at times it was touch and go. There were a few conversations where funders withdrew money. But it came down to this: we had a vision and strategy that justified the investment and donors believed and invested in us."

They also have a second rule that complements the first: they don't accept funding if a potential funder could become a defendant in their legal work. Devon says, "These commitments have been meaningful to our donors and have helped our funding. We are a principled organization and so our funding policy has to be principled. Donors think that distinguishes us."

Impact is the bottom line

Devon recognizes many charities struggling to stay afloat may have to allow donors to play a larger role in determining strategy. At the same time, he says he tells executive directors in other parts of the social good sector, "If you're determining your activities based on the appetite of your donors, how do you know you're making strategic choices? How would a funder know how you maximize your impact?"

Impact is the bottom line for strategy, Devon says. He also recognizes that measuring impact in environmental law is challenging unless Ecojustice gets a clear win in court. "That's the value of a strategic plan," he says. "After our cases, we assess whether we achieved our intended goals and we flow them back up the strategic plan to see whether our operations got us where we intended or not."

He also recognizes a different kind of impact: the impact of funding. "We have to have a vision that's independent of money, but we are also limited by our budget. Growing our budget has given us greater capacity to maximize our strategic impact. The reality is that it takes money to be able to move past sustainability and into thriving as an organization. I admire small organizations that are impactful within a small budget but it's really hard."

The challenge of innovation

Innovation is a big challenge within strategy, Devon says. "We struggle a lot with people being over-cautious, and innovation is an active conversation for us. You don't know what you don't know, and you get comfortable. It's difficult to move out of your lane to innovate." He adds, "We've often worked on building people's skills without talking about the overcautious culture."

There are places within any organization that require new responses. For Devon, chief among these are reconciliation and justice, equity, diversity, and inclusion. "We have a goal of enculturating these and

STRATEGY

it's a worthy goal. How that will be manifested is currently beyond our comprehension."

This takes Devon back to the shifts necessitated by COVID. "It's a shock that allowed us to find a different way of thinking, strategizing, and operating. Being cautious is self-limiting, so we are having concurrent conversations about audacious goals and doing what we do well now."

STRATEGY

Eden Grodzinski

Eden Grodzinski is the CEO of Habitat for Humanity Halton-Mississauga-Dufferin. Prior to that, she worked with municipalities and charitable organizations providing strategic guidance on issues related to affordable housing, homelessness, and other social determinants of health. I supported Eden and her Habitat affiliate with their recent strategic plan, and have worked with her on a variety of other community-building projects for many years.

Fixed and flexible

Eden believes the metaphor of elasticity describes her work well, although not simply because of COVID. "Things had to change. Affordable housing has become more and more difficult to find over the past decade, especially in the region where I serve. Environmental constraints such as land prices and building costs meant we had to pivot, but we are also serving different people now as low-income working poverty looks different than it used to. COVID has only accelerated the need to shift the conversation."

It is not only the stretch of an elastic that resonates with Eden but also the need to maintain a firmly rooted point from which to stretch. "In some matters, I have no say over what's fixed. I'm part of a larger federation and I can't change its history, mission, or some historical ways of operating. I have no say over housing prices in our market and I have to stay within CRA articles in terms of selling homes at a fair-market price." But, she adds, "I'm also trying to keep some things fixed by choice."

Chief among these fixed points is mission. Eden says, "You need to deeply understand your organization's mission and stay true to it. For us, a question we ask is: *will it serve more families?* We also consider the return on investment and whether an opportunity is in our wheelhouse.

STRATEGY

STRATEGY

Eden Grodzinski
Photographer: Hilary Gauld

If the answers are no, we say no. You have to be okay in being narrow in what you do."

Understanding this, she says, allows her to be strategic in choosing where and how to stretch. In her context, her organization has traditionally focused on home ownership, a model Eden says works best for families with children seeking to break the poverty cycle. She also considers whether there are other ways of achieving the same mission and offering the same benefits of homeownership in a context where land and housing costs make home ownership less accessible. They need to find other pathways to achieving the stability and financial equity that have traditionally come through buying a home.

Other more operational changes also need to be considered through the lens of mission. Habitat ReStores have historically been strong revenue engines for the organization. During lockdowns, this continued and even grew, but the ReStores also pivoted to selling through Facebook Marketplace. The role of volunteers with Habitat has also shifted. As a result of COVID, corporate teams of 50 were less likely to come to work on a build site, but the organization also began to rethink the role of volunteers in general. "Having volunteers on build sites is wonderful for community engagement and awareness raising, but it doesn't solve the problem of affordable housing. Our mission isn't about providing volunteer opportunities but empowering working lower income families to build strength, stability, and independence through affordable housing. We need to find a way to leverage our volunteers and still stay focused on our strategic goals of delivering more affordable units faster and at lower costs for families in need."

Mission drift

At times in any organization, it can be easy to drift from mission, especially when opportunities look appealing or come with significant revenue. "The success of our ReStores is an example of this," Eden says. "For a while, our organization became ReStore-oriented, and we had to say, 'No, we're firstly a housing organization. Our stores are an effective social enterprise that provides for our mission, but we are not a retail company.'"

She also firmly believes: "If your mission is good and you stick to it, the money will come."

To shift the metaphor, Eden says, "If you know your destination, you'll find a way to get there. You'll identify the roads that take you there, and if one is blocked, either you'll choose a different road or you'll get rid of the blocks." Mission drift can also come when people panic because they aren't on a road that's getting them where they want to go. "At those times, sticking to the mission helps you know you're not on the right road and allows you to correct your course in a timely way, but it also lets you trust the destination is still a good one."

Getting rid of the blocks does not simply mean pivoting or changing. In Eden's case, getting rid of the blocks can mean government advocacy or other ways of addressing the barriers to mission while staying true to it.

How a strategic plan fits

When people hear strategic, they often think strategic plans, and Eden says they aren't wrong to see the value in such plans.

What a strategic plan offers, Eden says, is purpose and clarity. "A strategic plan helps an organization take stock and get real data. Accurate level setting helps avoid drift and gives leaders conviction about their plan because they can see a full and clear picture." She adds that it is important to "measure what matters" when doing strategic planning as it will shape what people in the organization care about.

Eden has written many strategic plans as a consultant in the past and could have written her organization's strategic plan herself, but she brought in an external consultant for the organization's most recent strategic plan. "I could have written it myself," she says, "but I'm not a neutral party. The process of developing a strategic plan is important and it's vital to get buy-in from all stakeholders. An external consultant could have challenging conversations and push back in ways that an internal person, however skilled, just can't. They also provide validity and can talk about how other organizations have addressed similar opportunities and challenges." She adds that the recent process has given her more clarity and fresh ideas about how to work in her organization.

We can't be strategic alone

Strategic plans are only as good as their implementation, Eden says, recalling how she used to worry that strategic plans she did for clients would simply sit on a shelf. She has taken the strategic plan and built an operational template she uses in consultation with senior leaders in her organization, asking them to develop a work plan that addresses all goals—not just those specific to them. This is an approach she used in another housing organization where the goal was focused around ending homelessness, but the organization also had some responsibility for evictions. "We had to bring teams together to understand how all our purposes were working toward the same goal so what one division (evictions) was doing was not contradicting another (ending homelessness). This means a shift from a siloed approach to a collaborative one."

Often, the leader is the only person who sees all the parts of their organization at the 20,000-foot level, but they can't implement strategy alone. Eden reflects on her sports-playing sons, one of whom relies on his brute strength to score while the other kicks the ball where it needs to go but relies on someone being able to receive it. "You can't be strategic alone," Eden says. "It's my job to help others lift their gaze and see how their work functions as part of the broader organization, but I also need to find people who understand and share the vision."

Eden's board is a strong partner in this as it is a strategic board with a desire for change to accomplish their mission. She is also developing creative community partnerships, including with certain developers who are interested in sharing a vision for affordable housing.

"To quote one of my staff," Eden says, "We're still Habitat, but we're not your mother's Habitat!"

TRUST

Dr. Sidney Kennedy and Heather Froome

Sidney is the Executive Director of the Homewood Research Institute, and is also a professor of psychiatry, a world-renowned leader, and a sought-after speaker in his field. Heather is the Director of Operations at the Homewood Research Institute. She has previously worked as a leader in regional government, university, and community services.

Integrity and competence

The Homewood Health Centre (HHC) began almost 140 years ago in Guelph, Ontario and has since grown to a national suite of mental health and addiction services, including Ravensview in Victoria, British Columbia and a network of outpatient services across Canada. About 20 years ago, they established a separate research entity which is the nonprofit Homewood Research Institute (HRI). The two organizations continue to work closely together on key projects.

"This relationship takes trust," says Heather. "There's a lot of junk science out there. Homewood's CEO trusts that we have secured the right scientists with the right stature to work with their patients and clinical

Heather Froome and Dr. Sidney Kennedy
Photographer: Hilary Gauld

data." Sid says, "Integrity is vital for trust. There has to be a skillset and an area of expertise for others to come along."

Sid and Heather point to two leaders whose integrity and competence inspired trust in others in the formation of their research institute. Sid says, "I was impressed by the Schlegel family who are the drivers of the whole enterprise. Ron Schlegel and his commitment to research was a magnet for me. Ron is recognized as a business leader, but he earned a PhD and had a distinguished academic career. He is still academically curious and passionate about applied research."

Heather was attracted to working at HRI because of "the vision, honesty, and credibility of the former executive director who had led cancer research for years and was keen and committed to doing for mental health what has been done in cancer research."

That foundational integrity attracted others who added further credibility. "The former executive director sought out the scientists who were the best-known in the areas of trauma, addiction, and evaluation," Heather says. "They in turn became the magnets to attract top students and staff because people wanted to work with them. That gave Homewood confidence in us."

Organizational and personal interwoven

Years ago, at a party celebrating another research organization, someone asked Sid how his network had thrived for 20 years. Sid replied, "We know the wallpaper in each other's houses, whose kid is at which university." He adds, "Trust is about personal connection. And then if you represent an organization, it has to appear to be a trustworthy place, too."

The former executive director of HRI began his recruitment strategy in the Homewood cafeteria, learning about people's most urgent needs. He then invited potential researchers to Homewood for a kind of test-drive

TRUST

model where both sides could determine whether they were a fit for the institute.

"You have to find the right people and put them in the right seats on the bus," says Heather, "which is why personal relationships go a long way." She also believes a key to finding the right people is being upfront from the start about what an organization is looking for. In HRI's context, where collaboration is a key value, she says, "When someone is nominated as a collaborating scientist, we ask about whether they collaborate well and the agreement that follows outlines expectations for working in this way."

Sid says, "The world today is moving toward shared databases and international networks. You can do research on your own, but will end up with less and have less impact." He adds, "There's a small minority of researchers who fear their data and best ideas will be stolen and wouldn't touch networks. They vote with their feet. But the majority feel they are gaining [from collaboration]. Our networks have succeeded because of trust and personal connection."

That trust is built not simply in language but in action. An example of this is HRI's manuscript writing group where scientists, clinicians and staff meet biweekly with post-doctoral students to share their writing on a variety of topics related to addiction. "This teaches post-docs that this is an effective way to work," says Heather. Sid adds, "It's early imprinting for their careers."

Sid says that having loyalty to a shared values system and belief in mission builds trust. "Loyalty to why we're here gives us a sense of hope that we will move the needle on mental health, and it helps us to enjoy what we do even in difficult times," says Sid.

Having the base of trusted relationships and collaboration with integrity, Sid says, means that someone having a bad day does not disrupt the progress of the work, and that even critical feedback can be well received.

TRUST

Communication knits relationships together

HRI has a small staff but a wide and broad network of partners and stakeholders—funders, clinicians, scientists, students, post-doctoral fellows, staff, people with lived expertise, and government connections, among others. That means, as Heather says, "We spend a lot of time navigating relationships and knitting things together."

One of the key strands in that knitting process is that of continuous and honest communication in order to build and maintain trust. Sid says, "HRI does trust well. I've seen the difference in the broader research community." He recalls a recent conversation with a group of researchers presenting at an online HRI event where they reviewed logistics and needs. "They said to us they'd never had such a trusting and professional experience before."

"If you want to solve big problems and move forward in an intelligent manner," says Heather, "you need to allow all the sightlines on the problem. Good honest communication is what allows that and what helps get different people to row together in the same direction."

Sweet spot of overlapping interests

Trust is built on having shared goals and mission. "Sometimes," Heather says, "you can find the sweet spot through mutually reinforcing activities that are a win-win for all."

Sid says he learned how this works in the context of the relationship between academics and the pharmaceutical or device industries. "A lot of people look negatively at those researchers who work with industry, but I start by recognizing that industry goals might be to develop a drug that works and is a financial 'block-buster,' while my aspiration would be to publish a paper about that drug development. I understand there will be certain things they want that I won't do, and that there may be things I want—like a quicker turnaround—that they can't or won't deliver. But we can still develop a common ground."

TRUST

He says understanding this concept allows him to work and build trust with other organizations, including Homewood. "Our raison d'être is different than theirs and there are times when we have to recognize that we have different agendas. But we also have significant overlapping interests. Again, it comes down to mutual trust as the essential ingredient of any successful partnership."

TRUST

The Counselling Collaborative of Waterloo Region

The Counselling Collaborative of Waterloo Region emerged more than 15 years ago through the joint effort of six not-for-profit community counselling agencies in Waterloo Region. In 2018, through a strategic planning process I led, they moved to a significantly more integrated approach of working together to best serve the mental health needs of all residents in their community. They use a "no wrong door" approach and a centralized intake to help people connect with the member agencies and beyond. Sounds more straightforward than it has been in practice!

How trust begins to be built

While I could have talked with any one of the leaders from the six member agencies about their own elasticity and ways of working collaboratively, they suggested, instead, that it would be best to join one of their biweekly Executive Directors' Tea and Strategy meetings to talk about trust. When two of the six directors had scheduling conflicts, they were careful to find ways for those voices to be included.

This is not how counselling agencies in the same community typically operate, nor is it how these agencies have always worked. Initially, the group was brought together by the regional government to provide services to specific underserved groups of people, meeting quarterly to talk about programming. When other common funding opportunities emerged, their established relationships enabled communication and mutual problem solving. Then, in 2018, they initiated a strategic planning process that sparked more deliberate ways of working together. But the process wasn't always smooth.

Tracy Elop, CEO of Carizon Family and Community Services was a

Counselling Collaborative of Waterloo Region

Front Row, L to R: Cameron Dearlove (Porchlight Counselling and Addictions Services), Amanda Wood-Atkinson (Woolwich Counselling Centre), Rebecca Webb (KW Counselling Centre). Back Row, L to R: Matthew Isert Bender (Interfaith Counselling Centre), Lisa Akey (Carizon Family and Community Services), Susan Schwartzentruber (Shalom Counselling Services)

Photographer: Hilary Gauld

fairly new member to the group at the time. She describes the process, "When we started the strategic planning together, in my head, it seemed like a natural thing to do. I had secured some funding and was excited about it, but when I came forward with the idea, I was surprised that this excitement wasn't shared by everyone."

The problem was one of trust. Tracy continues, "I realized that I didn't have credibility with the other leaders. I was a finance person working with social workers who didn't think I knew what I was talking about. And, when I thought about it, perhaps I didn't." That acknowledgement helped turn the corner. "It was really important for me to come forward and to admit that I'd made a mistake, that I would take the hit with the funder if needed." Amanda Wood-Atkinson, who became the new Executive Director of Woolwich Counselling Centre in March 2020, reflects on these earlier stages of the collaborative, and acknowledges the challenges that the original leaders were facing. "Collaboration takes work," she says, "Trust takes work. The individual agencies had to make choices and have challenging conversations to think about what they were willing to support in order to better provide for the community."

A key factor in the transformation from individual agency to trusted partner was the facilitation process itself. The region had always been supportive of a collaborative approach and joined in the work to develop a strategic plan. Tracy reflects, "Key to the process was keeping us focused on our collective mission because if you believe everyone comes with the same goal, you can go a long way."

The strategic planning sessions led to a roadmap of where the collaborative could go. What that journey would look like, however, still needed to be negotiated. The leadership team at that time was made up of six strong, community-minded, passionate leaders. Emotions ran high at times. Diane McGregor, Counselling Collaborative Project Lead, remembers the level of emotional risk and vulnerability braved by these leaders at that time. She observes, "There were times when voices were raised

TRUST

and people felt genuinely hurt, but not a single person left the room. There was a willingness to hang in there, and a strong commitment to work it through."

Naming and sharing power

"Naming and sharing power were other important elements in building trust," says Cameron Dearlove, Executive Director of Porchlight Counselling and Addictions Services. He acknowledges the power imbalance between member agencies, due, in part, to their differences in size and scale, as well as their connectedness within the broader community.

Matthew Isert Bender, Executive Director of Interfaith Counselling Services, agrees, noting, "Carizon, one of our two largest agencies, functionally plays the role of the lead agency in the collaborative without actually acting like a lead agency." He adds, "That builds trust because nothing is dictated, and every member feels valued."

Rebecca Webb, Executive Director of KW Counselling Services, notes that, "To facilitate a true collaboration, we come at all decisions with a consensus approach where all have an equal voice, regardless of the size of their agency. That also goes a long way to building trust."

Amanda agrees: "My organization, by comparison, is tiny but I feel like I have an equal voice and the autonomy to opt in or out according to what's best for us." Amanda describes one decision that didn't make sense for her agency and says, "When I explained this, they gave me their full blessing to act as I needed. That deep respect for one another speaks well to how we manage the power differentials."

Cameron also agrees, recalling how his agency hit a rough patch in operations and finance not long after he joined the collaborative. "I felt like we were the weakest link," he says. But, unlike other groups he has been part of, where the power imbalance was never acknowledged and decisions were not actually shared, he says, "Very quickly I could sense from this group that there was openness to being vulnerable and willingness to offer options to provide support." He adds, "Now, when one of us meets a funder or a government minister, we trust that they will represent us as a broader collaborative. This is so refreshing because it's not often the experience. I know significant work went into this."

A precedent of stretching

Most of the leaders who were there at the formation of the collaborative and throughout the initial strategic planning process have retired or gone on to other roles, but they've left a legacy for those who followed.

Amanda says, "The initial stretching of our predecessors didn't come without pain. It's interesting to come in as a newer leader because you hear stories of what that was like, when strong leaders come together and each one has their own successful way of doing things."

Tracy affirms this, "When I think about the stretch that was required at the beginning of the collaborative, it went beyond the typical stretching within our own organizations, in our efforts to be the best we could be. It took a philosophical stretch where we had to recognize we could serve the community better together than we could on our own."

Better together

Indeed, the group lists a wide variety of ways they are better together. Amanda describes the biweekly virtual Tea and Strategy meetings (which began two weeks after her March 2020 start) as a lifeline. Matthew, who started around the same time, saw these meetings as an important way of getting onboarded and addressing any feelings of being overwhelmed as a new ED. Given the challenges of the pandemic, even veteran leaders like Tracy say, "If there were any lingering questions of trust and vulnerability, the urgency of COVID cemented relationships. We had to figure out how to support clients and help each other." Matthew says, "We can laugh together—it takes trust to joke with each other, but humour is part of trust." Amanda adds, "This is a meeting I try not to miss. I have this

TRUST

group I trust deeply who will give honest answers." Cameron also notes that the meetings offer opportunity to discuss and get help with specific practical concerns, such as contracts and budgets.

Susan Schwartzentruber, Executive Director of Shalom Counselling Services comments, "We see each other as a resource and support because leadership roles can be isolating. We respect the uniqueness of each agency and the various services we provide to the community. Our discussions build on our strengths and our differences are valued rather than defended."

For smaller agencies, working collaboratively also allows access to resources and greater levels of advocacy that would otherwise be impossible. But all agree, "When we look at where we've gotten to and the results we've achieved together for the community, there's no way one agency could have done it alone." It has meant clearer navigation for clients through a shared phone number, website, centralized intake process, and service navigation. It has also meant shared staff and services, including the project lead. Lisa Akey, Director of Counselling and Carizon's current representative on the Leadership Team states, "We have also attracted multiple sources of funding we wouldn't otherwise have. We have a reputation in the community and our credibility has increased. Our community partners can trust us as a true collaboration, working together."

This approach also extends beyond their local community, with one of their provincial funders noting that this approach is creative, innovative, and cost-effective, and it is a potential model for other jurisdictions.

Lisa sums it up, "The outcomes have made it all worthwhile."

IMAGINATION

Julia Grady

Julia Grady is the co-founder and Executive Director of Guelph's 10C, a not-for-profit social enterprise creating a platform for those working across sectors and engaging in collaborative work to improve community. Julia is a working encaustic artist and community finance innovator who ran her own web development business. As a resident of the city that Julia makes better, I sincerely appreciate her community building superpowers!

We aren't imaginative enough

"The reason I'm on this planet," says Julia, "is to be creative, imaginative, heart-led, and thinking of how things could be different and experimenting and trying to make those things happen." For Julia, her work as a placemaker with 10C is rooted in her identity as an artist. "Artists are flexible and intuitive. We're always looking and wayfinding but also responding and shifting as things unfold."

At the same time, Julia thinks imagination itself is under-imagined by people across sectors. "When you read about business strategy, the word imagination doesn't come up. People think and talk strategy, but they

Julia Grady
Photographer: Hilary Gauld

don't realize that imagination, passion, and creativity are actually the underlying ideas and principles in the top companies in the world."

"I don't think we collectively imagine enough," Julia says. "Too often we're afraid to imagine and dream bigger than we are. We assume certain things are impossible because they don't exist yet."

But that is exactly where Julia and 10C operate.

She tells the origin story of 10C which began in Guelph after she and her co-founder observed that many groups of people working for social good in Guelph didn't even know about each other, let alone have a place where they could meet and cross-pollinate. 10 Carden Street was the original location of what was a co-working/meeting space. From that beginning, the organization grew and evolved around the question that drove their imaginative vision: what do changemakers need?

"When you imagine what could be possible and hold that vision collectively, the steps and the pieces become clear and it's easy to get where you're going." She clarifies this to add, "Seeing solutions is easy, but it's a lot of hard work to implement, try things, and see if they meet needs." Recognizing the need for a more accessible physical space led 10C to purchase a large old furniture store; recognizing the need for capital to purchase and renovate that space led 10C to build a bigger membership and from those people raise $2.3M in community bonds over a three-year period. They developed a commercial kitchen in response to needs from members, an asset that continued to provide income during COVID lockdowns that shifted their placemaking model in some other ways.

"Artists are actually often entrepreneurial," says Julia, "because we're used to making something out of nothing or using what we have. 10C is driven by the same skills you would use with a blank canvas. It is entirely a creative process in connecting and communicating in the world." Today, 10C operates with a staff of 20 and about 250 community memberships, 40,000 square feet of social purpose real-estate, and numerous social change projects.

IMAGINATION

How to imagine

Julia returns to the art world to describe how to imagine, saying she pictures the work of 10C as being like a three-dimensional and living web with multiple connections between different points on the web.

Regardless of the type of work anyone is engaged in, Julia says, art offers a way of imagining. "Often, we think of problems as a negative thing, but for an artist, design constraints are a useful container in which to operate. And many problems have embedded solutions when they are considered together." She looks at the creative solution that came out of an inaccessible building and a costly redevelopment of a historic building into a new, accessible site as jumpstarting them into new and exciting possibilities.

When the question of COVID lockdowns arises, Julia isn't even interested in going there. Instead, she says, "I'm always looking for what's going on under the surface." Like the opportunities that came out of having to move from an inaccessible building, 10C approached COVID as a design constraint that shifted their work in some ways but still addressed their core vision of resilient and sustainable communities and supporting people to do good things. During COVID, programs and building forward new social infrastructure became 10C's driving work.

In addition to continuing to grow their social finance tools at a time when other funding opportunities were fewer, 10C saw the opportunity in the changes COVID caused to their local farmers' market. Prior to the pandemic, the market was rethinking its business model to drive increased engagement and utilization. The closure of that market during spring 2020 amplified this goal. 10C responded to a subsequent call for proposals from the city to become the 'activator of the market.' "We didn't have our own plan for the market," Julia says, "but we knew we could activate the conversation and help craft a vision of what that space could be." This is what they're embarking on now.

IMAGINATION

Change

"We don't have to reinvent the wheel," Julia says, "but we do need to change when something doesn't serve us anymore." This is where imagination can feel scary. "We don't know how it will be, but if we try something, we gain more courage to do things in the next round."

This is true even when change means getting smaller or when change comes as a response to failure or when change is needed after a long season of success.

"If we don't keep trying new and imaginative things, we will do the same and easy things. But we can do hard things," Julia counsels, observing that the most creative people are often those who have experienced hard things in their lives but who remain tenacious and willing to learn.

When considering how to change, she says, we balance the benefits of the past with an ability to keep imagining the future. When 10C is deciding between possible ideas, Julia strives to look to what might be needed in the future: "We ask, 'What makes the most sense right now?' And then we say, 'what if we could...?' and we apply a bit of imagination to the how and the who could be involved." This involves thinking about infrastructure, whether that is building skills in staff that can be transferable to working with another organization, thinking about space that can be used by multiple groups on a regular basis, or considering whether an idea would be better accomplished by or in collaboration with another group.

Imagining together

Julia says she yearns for more collective imagination because "That will be where and how all kinds of organizations, businesses, and individuals working for good can make communities better."

This kind of conversation, she says, can have a lot of different openings where people and organizations look at challenges and imagine together what a future might look like. She recognizes that some imaginative

IMAGINATION

people, like her, are inclined to jump ahead rather than engage in the longer process of bringing people alongside to imagine together. This is where having someone lead the conversation and invite collaborators together can be useful.

Another factor in imagining together involves funders. For Julia, social financing is a passion. "The money is already out there. It is simply being deployed in ways that cause harm to people and the planet. Organizations need to be innovative around growing social impact work that earns revenue, and this is important because nonprofits have the most to offer the world right now."

IMAGINATION

Jennifer Hutton

Jennifer Hutton is the CEO at Women's Crisis Services of Waterloo Region (WCSWR) where she formerly served as Outreach Manager. She has also worked in a hospital setting. Jennifer holds two master's degrees, in social work and in business. She's also an avid Toronto Blue Jays fan. She considers being a mom to her currently five-year-old daughter to be her most important role. I appreciated working with Jennifer and her team on their strategic plan. The process and product were memorable to me because they made things very visual.

The elastic has been stretched too far. We need to celebrate.

"It may sound dramatic, but I've seen in our work that the elastic has been stretched too far," says Jennifer. "The people we are supporting have much more complex needs than before. Across the province, shelters are having trouble finding staff. That means not only are front-line staff burned out but so are our leaders."

As CEO of Women's Crisis Services of Waterloo Region, Jennifer says, "I'm gritty and I have the usual coping skills because I know I have to keep stretching and being agile." This stretchiness and agility requires imagination. "I am constantly thinking about what could help, what could the next idea be, what could we try next. We try something, reflect on how it worked, and change constantly."

She also celebrates when ideas work. Jennifer says, "Our work can be hard because we don't always see immediate gratification. But the more we focus on the good, the more that will expand." In response to a growing leadership team that may feel somewhat disconnected, Jennifer is initiating a Teams chat to share moments of gratitude. She also reflects on a recent project that brought the whole team together—renovating a

IMAGINATION

Jennifer Hutton
Photographer: Hilary Gauld

triplex to become transitional housing in a short period of time. "So many people were involved in thinking about how to do it, and then literally tearing down walls and pulling it together. It was so gratifying when it all came together and we pulled it off."

Imagining together is better than imagining alone

While Jennifer says, "I always was that kid with my head in the clouds doing imaginative things, and I love doing that in our work now," she does not operate in a model where the CEO sets the vision and the staff implement it. "Imagination done collectively makes all the difference—we're better together. I might throw out ideas, and then others ask questions and build on it, and something new emerges."

A beautiful example of this is the "She Is Your Neighbour" campaign. Jennifer describes the process through which this idea emerged. "One day, our senior director, our fundraiser, and I were brainstorming in the office. One person said that women who were abused were in the shadows and that people wanted to look away from what they thought they would see. But we knew abuse can touch anyone. Someone said the phrase, 'She is your neighbour,' and we ran with it." This campaign began with a blog series and bus shelter ads with real faces of local women who had experienced violence, including a former mayor. The campaign evolved into a popular podcast that includes voices of prominent Canadians speaking about abuse. More than three years later, this campaign continues to grow and be well-received.

Imagining together is enhanced by a team with a diverse set of skills and aptitudes. Jennifer says, "We play off each other, knowing where people's strengths are."

She observes, "Sometimes, because we have ideas and because opportunities present themselves, we spread ourselves too thin." Not only does she depend on the team to help, but she and the team together rely on their strategic plan to guide their choices about which plans to pursue.

IMAGINATION

Take time for conversations

Like the "She Is Your Neighbour" campaign, many of the best ideas emerge in conversation. While some might wonder whether conversation slows the process down, Jennifer says, "We've had evidence that time is well spent in conversation. Sometimes, a pivotal conversation can send you down an important path forward." Such a conversation occurred during a recent strategic planning session. "We were working on an illustration of the pillars of our work, and someone included the phrase 'more than shelter.' This phrase had come out of conversations with our community partners who said that people thought of us only as a shelter. While that is our unique proposition, we offer a menu of services. We aren't just a warm meal and a bed. Rebecca suggested we put that phrase front and centre. We now incorporate it into our communications, hashtag it on our social media, and do a blog series on it. I put a large illustration of the phrase in our shelters where people see it every day."

Some pivotal conversations even save time. During a break in programming at a leadership planning session, managers began discussing the challenges in their work. Conversation about one of the biggest common challenges—spending too much time tweaking schedules—led to the emergence of a solution (hiring a contract scheduler) that has significantly reduced the time managers spend on this activity.

Be willing to try

Vulnerability is a hallmark of both the clients and the staff of WCSWR, many of whom are survivors of domestic violence themselves. It's important to Jennifer that her team is aware their vulnerability is welcome. This means, as Jennifer says, "We work hard to free our team up from perfectionism and to let them know it's okay to make mistakes." In the ideation process, Jennifer strives to model this. "At times, I have to say, 'This was my idea and it didn't work out.'"

Sometimes, vulnerability is not about mistakes but living out the consequence of choices. "When we started our blog series, the 'defund the police' issue was beginning—and we are connected to the police. That became an issue on social media. Part and parcel with us being creative and getting known in the community on social media is that it can come with critique."

Vulnerability also shows up in bridging the common divide between frontline staff and leaders by resisting the urge to fix, and instead inviting other voices in. "As a leader, I have to remember to step back and say: 'What do you think we could do?'" Jennifer says, recalling the recent contest to name their transitional house. "One of our newer frontline staff gave a brilliant and meaningful response with the name Aspen, explaining how aspen trees grow together and shield each other. When we shared the name with the board, it brought one member to tears. It reminded me of the richness of our frontline staff."

One of the biggest risks paid off in helping serve clients. Jennifer tells the story: "Early in the pandemic, people weren't reaching out to us for help. This surprised and worried us. We quickly realized people weren't reaching out because they couldn't—our clients would normally call when their partner was out, and under lockdown they didn't have a safe way to do that." Within 48 hours, they had created an online chat feature so clients could discreetly type a message asking for support. Jennifer says, "It didn't have to be perfect, but we had to try something. We said, 'Here's the problem, here's a solution,' and we got it up."

IMAGINATION

CURIOSITY

Dorothy Nyambi

Dr. Dorothy Nyambi is the President and CEO at Mennonite Economic Development Associates. She is also the chair of the International Development Research Centre in Ottawa. Before this, she was the Executive Vice President at the African Institute for Mathematical Sciences—Next Einstein Initiative and served in leadership in other charities during her career which began as a medical doctor serving in Cameroon and, later on, with the United States Peace Corps in multiple countries in the Global South.

Not cynical or surface

On her background in health, Dorothy says, "I really believe in working with people to unpack their own minds—that people have the solutions to their own problems—rather than assuming that medicine is magic." She adds, "I bring that same curious approach into my leadership work."

"In every situation, I give people the benefit of the doubt. In order to lead, you have to get people to come along." She adds that rather than being cynical, she brings a sense of curiosity to challenges: "What is driving them? What is holding them back? What am I doing that is leading to this behaviour?"

Dorothy Nyambi
Photographer: Hilary Gauld

Her belief that people have the solutions to their own problems is connected with an understanding that change starts within and at home. She says, "I tend to very quickly check myself and who I am and what I can control in a situation." As she works to develop a North-South shift in a development subsector dominated by explicit and implicit racism, white 'saviourism,' and sexism, she says, "I have been pushed to my limits but not past. There is a lot of resistance to me as a female Black leader." Dorothy says, however, that change in terms of equity, diversity, and inclusion can't simply be made through workplace diversity training. "People need to go home and figure out their own self and build out their own personal circles so that change is not just cosmetic, but that people come to work as different people."

Risk failing

"If we want to build a culture of curiosity," Dorothy says, "we have to risk failure. I cultivate agency in my direct reports, letting them know it is okay to fail and to look at our failures. I remind them that the organization is elastic, so you can fail without breaking the organization." She adds, "We don't want to spend all our time failing, but we have to learn to incentivize willingness to fail." She observes that western culture tends to take a stance of appreciation where "if it ain't broke, don't fix it." By contrast, she says, "I ask: how can we do better?"

Dorothy describes a recent encouraging example of this. "We made two mistakes in two grant proposals. In many organizations, people would cover this up and hide it from the CEO, but I was encouraged and excited that the person within whose team this happened brought it to my attention immediately, knowing I would not hold it against him and knew we could do better next time." A resilient and successful organization is one in which this behaviour and culture transcends through all levels. She adds, "Where I have failed with the board or the organization, I've owned

CURIOSITY

that. I've also told my direct reports to hold me accountable when they have concerns and, trust me, they do."

"I want to build a culture where competence is not about looking good but about being authentic and honest about how things actually are and how we can keep improving while moving on."

Behaviour not words

"There's a lot of talk about curiosity, but in the real world, that doesn't always translate into behaviour," Dorothy says.

One place where Dorothy sees this most clearly is in the talk about making sure colleagues in the Global South can bring their voices to the table. "People say they are curious, but they also don't know how to give up power to be able to do so." She offers that, "After generations where nothing changed, where they have seen development workers come and go and pat themselves on the shoulder and nothing really changes, people in the Global South don't quite trust that those from the North are coming to the table with authenticity. It will take examples for them to know that we mean what we say." It is too easy, she observes, for people from the North to see themselves as specialists rather than recognizing that "the people closest to the challenge have better insights and should have responsibility in decision making and design for change." Even Dorothy herself, who was raised in the Global South, has to remind herself, "I have lived experience but those living it now have better ideas. We have to work together."

She also observes that people from all parts of the globe have deeply colonized minds while those in the South struggle with a sense of inferiority. Overcoming this, for Dorothy, requires curiosity about her own mind and reflection on her own experience, and then sharing that with others so they can do the work of decolonization together. "I actively think about and realize the ways my own mind is colonized. If you don't recognize and own it, you cannot fix it. I'm also not shy about sharing my own experience. If I've experienced it, I've experienced it, and I will tell you how." In her own organization, she observes that the board hired her, welcoming a more diverse leadership, but it has been difficult for her to feel fully included. "Inclusion is a complex potpourri of factors that have to do with trust," she says. "It includes who gets included or sidelined, where the focus of power is within an organization."

Dorothy also believes her modeling of vulnerable feminist leadership where everyone can be a leader is a way of demonstrating a curious and decolonized mind.

Olympic team more than family

Dorothy cites an African proverb that has guided her work: "When many bees are coming at you, choose which one you will swat." For Dorothy, you swat the ones coming at your eyes so you can see what is ahead, prioritizing what to focus on.

It's for this reason that Dorothy rejects the metaphor of a staff team as a family, saying instead that they are like an Olympic team, where everyone has their strengths in service of the same goal.

Having Dorothy as a leader has been one of the biggest ways in which her organization has needed to be elastic in the last few years. Dorothy thinks one of the strengths she brings to her work is showing up as her honest self: "What you see is what you get. I bring myself and I will be honest and direct." At the same time, as on an Olympic team, she believes the goal is for the organization and its people to make themselves invisible in the service of the mission.

For this reason, she regrets not ensuring her whole team fully shared her vision when she began work in the organization. At the same time, she says, "I would not change our board. They had never stretched as they did or been tested as they have been, but they stood with me after hiring and helped me not to snap and by so doing, helped the organization. They have been collegial and exceptional."

CURIOSITY

Sandra Austin

Sandra is the Director of Strategic Initiatives for The Regional Municipality of Durham, Ontario, Canada. Her portfolio includes the Regional Strategic Plan and organizational performance, key policy work, climate action and environmental sustainability, government and community relations, and innovation. I have helped Sandra's team articulate their value proposition, and appreciated their early adoption of AQ assessments.

Start with why

"Our department's portfolio includes drastically different projects and files that don't fit neatly into other departments," says Sandra of her work for the Regional Municipality of Durham. "In fact, we have five distinct, high-priority and high-profile portfolios within my division." Further, in a municipal government space, Sandra says, "There's often a lot of change over a short period of time, and every change in circumstances requires us to adapt. How do we continue to adapt in situations where previous tactics might not work anymore?"

For Sandra and her team, it begins with curiosity. "We are always curious about why things are the way they are and then about how we might look at things from a different perspective." This means asking probing curious questions from the start ('Where do you see this going? Is this work we can add value to, or does it fit better elsewhere?'). That same curiosity drives the ability to be adaptable. "Governments are grappling with messy problems where we don't always know the outcome. We need to be comfortable with things being uncertain and moving into untried things, asking 'What if we did it this way?'"

But this is not merely curiosity for its own sake. "You don't want to drive those around you to the point of exhaustion because you want to

Sandra Austin
Photographer: Kirsten McGoey

change everything all the time." This is where Sandra talks about being anchored in the strategic plan as a way of defining key initiatives and timelines. "If there are rubs and frustrations, then you want to be curious about how to do that in a way people will accept." There will always be opportunities, but Sandra says that's not always the place to start. Rather, she says, "Start with the simple and straightforward question: 'what challenges us?'" She adds, "The more we understand the issues, the more that opens the door to asking curious questions about how things might be better. It's critical to addressing problems in an innovative way." As an example of this, Sandra talks about intelligent communities, and the difference between simply installing sensors on light standards, versus the challenge of how to ease traffic congestion and make communities safer and more accessible. "We begin with what needs addressing and then we consider what tools would address those needs, rather than the other way around."

Team curiosity

When Sandra's team engaged in the Adaptability Quotient, she says, "It helped us understand why not everyone approaches work the way we do. Our team scored exceptionally high on mental flexibility and the ability to 'unlearn,' but not everyone approaches problems by unpacking, deconstructing, and then putting the pieces back together. We realized, in fact, that while it's natural for many of our team members, for some people this approach causes frustration and fear."

But again, Sandra approaches even that fear with curiosity. "If there's discomfort with change or a mental block, we come back to asking why, and trying to understand."

That doesn't mean that resistance is wrong. Sandra says, "We need individuals who might be more risk averse. They're a critical part of the equation because they can shine a light on things that could go wrong or things we might have glossed over. It widens the lens."

Sandra also says that curiosity needs to be balanced with traditional measures of performance. "If it's all curiosity all the time, that leaves little time for the doing. At the end of the day, we are measured by what we accomplish."

But, despite these cautions and despite Sandra's awareness of hiring for a diversity of perspectives, she says, "A lot of what I look for when I hire members of our team are the elements of creativity they bring to their work. Are they open to looking at things in creative ways or are they following a textbook approach? Even with policy making, there are ways to approach things differently and we're constantly learning."

Once such people are hired, Sandra works to understand the context and conditions her staff members need to exercise their curiosity. Her team regularly holds 15-minute staff huddles where they come together to spark ideas, but she also protects the need for thinking time for those who do better with processing before engaging with others. Some people need to talk through items, while others observe and contemplate. She also deliberately cultivates psychological safety of sharing ideas with the team by sharing her own ideas, even if they are not fully formed, and encouraging others to do the same.

Is curiosity rewarded in your context?

"Many of my counterparts and colleagues face similar big-picture challenges, so there's always room for us to consider 'what if' questions to ask how we might look at things a bit differently, realign, or shift a conversation."

Sandra also describes an approach of focusing on "the coalition of the willing," saying, "There will always be resistance, so let's not spend energy pushing back but instead focus on finding willing partners and engaging with them. That has led us in incredible directions."

One example of this is their recently launched deep residential retrofit program that is the first of its kind in Canada. This initiative involves a

CURIOSITY

wide spectrum of partners but began with Sandra's department exercising curiosity in two ways. "We recognized that even if we did everything in our community energy plan, we would still fall short of achieving community greenhouse gas emissions reduction targets, so we asked: 'What else could we do? How can we empower residents to reduce their emissions as well?'" Sandra also says it was critical that the manager of sustainability who works for her department and leads this project "is more than an environmentalist, but has a business background as well so they can translate the benefits to business and industry and how they could work with us."

What are you curious about right now?

One of Sandra's portfolios is government-to-government relationships, which includes some Indigenous engagement. Sandra says, "For me, it's acknowledging the impacts of colonialism, and thinking, 'What can I do to be a good ancestor and use my position to support Indigenous peoples in my life and work?'" As we spoke, Sandra was preparing for a trip to a place in British Columbia that she knows has taken steps to incorporate Indigenous knowledge and perspectives. While she says she often takes an approach of observing and later researching answers to questions that arise, she says, "In this case, I'm going with specific questions. There is so much to learn from traditional ecological knowledge. Respecting and protecting natural spaces is critical to addressing climate change, so I'll be curious to understand the partnerships that have been developed, and how we can take similar approaches with local policy and projects."

CURIOSITY

PART FIVE

The Challenge

The person you are right now is as transient, as fleeting,
and as temporary, as all the people you've ever been.
~Dan Gilbert

SUMMATION

Now that you're almost at the end, I'm curious what will stick with you about this book. It feels presumptuous of me to summarize the key points for you. I would rather know what stood out from your perspective.

Here's what stands out for me:

- The metaphor of elasticity has maintained its resonance for me, throughout the writing of this book and even throughout the many faces and phases of pandemic and post-pandemic life. The need to stretch, the mysteries of what "too far for too long" look and feel like, leaving extra "give" as a buffer, and the frustration of being expected to reassume shapes that no longer suit me have become lenses through which I am starting to see the world.

- As for the acronym, its elements have become more dynamic for me over time. They are both inputs and outcomes, skills and currencies. They are experienced and improved both individually and collectively. Their interconnections defied a legible diagram.

- Given these overlaps, perhaps it is unsurprising that when you investigate how to grow each of the qualities included in this acronym, you get the sense that the lists of tips are all roughly the same. That's good news! A few well-chosen, high leverage habits can serve to strengthen multiple skills at once, like good nutrition, sleep, and exercise do. Sadly, it can seem like every good quality we can think of is listed and grouped under whatever category we're talking about (strategic leader is a trusted leader is a likeable leader... and they all demonstrate integrity, vulnerability, respect, good communication skills...).

- The people and organizations excelling in this space embody the overlaps. The folks chosen to showcase one skill in the case studies could easily have been slotted into one of the others. As you improve in one area, the others are likely to get stronger too.

APPLICATION

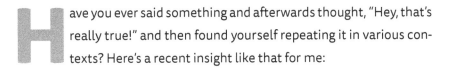

Have you ever said something and afterwards thought, "Hey, that's really true!" and then found yourself repeating it in various contexts? Here's a recent insight like that for me:

Knowing about something
doesn't reap the benefits of doing it.

Now you know about elasticity, physically and metaphorically. You know the elements of the acronym ELASTIC(ISH) and hopefully have caught a glimpse of the interconnections between them. You've been introduced to people working to put these skills into practice.

So now what?

What would it take for these insights to result in improvements in your life?

What we learn gets embedded more deeply the sooner we act on it. If you find it helpful to be told what to do, here are a few first steps.

First, develop a clear sense of where you are and where you'd like to be, using the ELASTIC metaphor, acronym, and inspirational examples as your guides. What skills do you want to learn? Where do you need to stretch more, less, or in different directions? As Lewis Carroll's Cheshire Cat is famous for saying, "If you don't know where you're going, any road will take you there."

Stop reading, grab a journal, scratch pad, or iPad and write down your intention. Now. Before reading any further.

Did you know that one root of the word intention means "to stretch?" According to the Webster Dictionary, an intention is "A stretching or bending of the mind toward an object; closeness of application; fixedness of attention; earnestness." So, get clear on your intention.

Then, pick one thing to start with. Choosing a focus and aiming for 1% improvement is more doable than trying to get better at every element of ELASTIC at once. (I know you know that. I also know that many of you are over-achievers who are going to try to get great at all of them simultaneously. Pick. One. Thing.) Read James Clear's *Atomic Habits*[341] for inspiration!

Next, check your mindset for limiting beliefs you are snapping back to already. It's time to channel Marcus Aurelius when he wrote, "What stands in the way becomes the way." For instance, are you discouraged by having tried to move the needle in this area in the past, such that you struggle to believe change is possible this time? What might it feel like to turn that persistent, stubborn thought pattern to your advantage? Could you reframe it to become some variation of "I am gritty and persistent?"

Beware that sometimes grit can make us bear down too hard (think of gritting your teeth!). Oliver Burkeman recounts stories of climbers who died on Mount Everest because they stuck with something too persistently for too long.[342] Yet we know that most leaders prefer testing over planning[343]—so try stuff! Adopt a posture of experimentation more than determination. Keep it light.

As you are experimenting with new ways of thinking and being, be careful who you listen to. As Brené Brown emphasizes in *Daring Greatly*, don't accept any feedback from the "cheap seats."[344] Instead, be inspired by the company you keep. As Ben Hardy says, "Never take advice from someone you wouldn't trade places with."[345]

Remember the power of collaboration and co-elevation over

competition. Think Yelp rather than Frommer's. In *New Power*, Heimans and Timms refer to the emergence of a "full stack society," where the different components of an operating system work together to make a product hum. How can you work together with others to advance your intentions and theirs? [346]

Finally, push the edges of your thinking. Play a bigger game. One provocative question Chip and Dan Heath pose in their book *Decisive* has stayed with me: "You can't choose any of the current options. What else could you do?"[347]

Rebecca Sutherns
Photographer: Hilary Gauld

INVITATION

Because strengthening our ELASTIC leadership skills is a group activity not just an individual one, I would like to invite you to continue learning about it in conversation with others.

A community of ELASTIC practitioners is emerging, and you're welcome to become a part of it. A first step would be to enroll in an ELASTIC leadership workshop series, or to host one in your workplace.

I'd welcome the opportunity to speak on ELASTIC skills at your upcoming conference or corporate retreat.

Have a look at the evolving gallery of ELASTIC case studies.

All of this can be found at **rebeccasutherns.com**.

Soon, we will be initiating a community of certified ELASTIC facilitators, equipped to guide others on their journey toward greater stretchiness. If this material has resonated with you and you'd like to incorporate it into your coaching practice, get in touch.

It is my hope that reading this book will stretch your thinking just enough, and that you will take action to embed that learning into your practice as soon as possible.

Gratitude

It takes a village to get a book out into the world, and I am immensely grateful to mine.

Laurie Watson is my practice manager. She took care of every detail along the way with speed, care and the attention to detail I often don't have. This book would not be in front of you without her.

Susan Fish is not only one of my best and longest friends, but also a gifted interviewer and writer. She handled the case studies beautifully.

Photographer Hilary Gauld made the case studies even more beautiful with her eye for taking stunning portraits. I am also grateful to Kirsten McGoey and Grace Robertson for stepping in when Hilary lived too far away to snap the shots herself.

To the colleagues who were willing to pose for those photos, to have a conversation with Susan and to put their lessons out for all to see, I am very grateful. As Hilary said to me afterwards, "You have the best clients!"—I really do.

Oliver Sutherns can always be counted on for clean and creative graphic design. His work complemented the team at Hambone Publishing wonderfully, and I appreciate the work that Ben, Mish and their crew did there. This is our third book together and we're definitely getting the hang of it!

There were people in five countries who read this manuscript and provided thoughtful feedback to make it stronger before it was released to a wider audience. I sincerely appreciate their time, candour, and insight.

Many of them also took the leap of being involved in the early ELASTIC workshops. Thank you to Sandra Allison, Sandra Austin, Jodi Ball, Glenna Banda, Stuart Beumer, Hannah Brown, Meredith Burpee, Adrienne Crowder, Kim Cusimano, Amanda Etches, Meeta Gandhi, Shane Hatton, Christine Hyde, Jennifer Juste, Ron Kadyschuk, Linda Kenny, Alicia King, Chad Littlefield, Karen Martin Schiedel, Anne McArthur, Lisa O'Neill, Marcia Scheffler, Katie Soles, Emily Stahl, Tim Sutherns, Ross Thornley, Mark Valcic, and Dave Whiteside.

I am also grateful to those who read my blog "wiser decisions faster" (rebeccasutherns.com/thoughts) each week and fill my inbox with challenging questions and encouragement. You sharpen my thinking and remind me that people are in fact reading what I'm putting out there. I am honoured by that.

And as always, the unwavering support of my husband Tim and each of my now-big kids is a gift I don't take for granted. And Tatum's welcome interruptions, and Remy's well-timed appearance just as this book was being finalized brighten my life more than they'll ever know.

*When we have the courage
to walk into our story and own it,
we get to write the ending.*
~Brené Brown[348]

References

1   Rebecca Sutherns. *Sightline: Strategic plans that gather momentum not dust.* (Hambone Publishing, 2020).

2   McKinsey & Company. *Building workforce skills at scale to thrive during—and after—the COVID-19 crisis (survey).* April 30, 2021. https://www.mckinsey.com/business-functions/people-and-organizational-performance/our-insights/building-workforce-skills-at-scale-to-thrive-during-and-after-the-covid-19-crisis

3   McKinsey & Company. *Defining the skills citizens will need in the future world of work.* June 2021. https://www.ic3institute.org/resourcelibrary/wp-content/uploads/2022/03/defining-the-skills-citizens-will-need-in-the-future-of-work-final.pdf

4   McKinsey & Company. *Future proof: Solving the 'adaptability paradox' for the long term.* August 2021. https://www.mckinsey.com/business-functions/people-and-organizational-performance/our-insights/future-proof-solving-the-adaptability-paradox-for-the-long-term

5   David Rock. *4 leadership trends to watch in 2022.* Fast Company. December 30, 2021. https://www.fastcompany.com/90704896/4-leadership-trends-to-watch-in-2022

6   David Rock. *4 leadership trends to watch in 2022.* Fast Company. December 30, 2021. https://www.fastcompany.com/90704896/4-leadership-trends-to-watch-in-2022

7   Brian D. Evans. *Most CEOs Read A Book A Week. This Is How You Can Too.* Inc.com. https://www.inc.com/brian-d-evans/most-ceos-read-a-book-a-week-this-is-how-you-can-too-according-to-this-renowned-.html

8   Chip Heath & Dan Heath. *Decisive: How to Make Better Choices in Life and Work* (Random House Canada, 2013).

9   John Pollack. *Shortcut: How Analogies Reveal Connections, Spark Innovation, and Sell Our Greatest Ideas* (Avery, 2014).

10 Bartosz Czekala. *The Truth about Effectiveness and Usefulness of Mnemonics in Learning.* Universe of Memory. https://universeofmemory.com/effectiveness-and-usefulness-of-mnemonics/

11 Tara Radović & Dietrich Manzey. *The Impact of a Mnemonic Acronym on Learning and Performing a Procedural Task and Its Resilience Toward Interruptions.* Frontiers in Psychology. November 2019. DOI: 10.3389/fpsyg.2019.02522.

12 Megan Mocko, Lawrence M. Lesser, Amy E. Wagler & Wendy S. Francis. *Assessing Effectiveness of Mnemonics for Tertiary Students in a Hybrid Introductory Statistics Course.* Journal of Statistics Education, 25(1): 2-11, 2017. DOI: 10.1080/10691898.2017.1294879.

13 Lisa Gerber. Personal Communication. August 2022. https://bigleapcreative.com/

14 Jason Thompson. Personal Communication. August 2022. https://www.jasonthompson.ca/storyist

15 Joe Alper. *Stretching the Limits.* Science, July 2002, vol 297, issue 5580, 329-331. DOI: 10.1126/science.297.5580.329.

16 Glenn Elert. *Elasticity, The Physics Hypertextbook.* https://physics.info/elasticity/

17 Ryan Holiday. *The Obstacle is the Way: The Ancient Art of Turning Adversity to Advantage* (Profile Books, 2015).

18 Scott Sonenshein. *Stretch: Unlock the Power of Less – and Achieve More Than You Ever Imagined* (Harper Business, 2017).

19 Mihaly Csikszentmihalyi. *Flow: The Psychology of Optimal Experience* (Harper Perennial Modern Classics, 2008).

20 Kelechi Udoagwu. *Top Tips for Setting Team Stretch Goals.* Wrike. June 2022. https://www.wrike.com/blog/setting-stretch-goals/#What-is-a-stretch-goal

21 Sim B. Sitkin, C. Chet Miller & Kelly E. See. *The Stretch Goal Paradox.* Harvard Business Reivew. January-February 2017. https://hbr.org/2017/01/the-stretch-goal-paradox

22 Adam Kahane. *Collaborating with the Enemy: How to Work with People You Don't Agree with or Like or Trust* (Berrett-Koehler Publishers, 2017).

23 Julia Galef. *The Scout Mindset: Why Some People See Things Clearly and Others Don't* (Penguin Publishing Group, 2021).

24 Chip Heath & Dan Heath. *The Power of Moments* (Simon & Schuster, 2017): 131

25 Jenn Skelton. *Flexibility Isn't What We Think It Is.* Repose. April 2018. https://reposelifestyle.com/2018/04/flexibility-isnt-what-we-think-it-is/

26 Frances Hutchens. *Stretching: You're Not Tight.* Movementum. 2019. https://movementum.co.uk/journal/2019/5/30/stretching

27 Jim Moss. Personal Communication. September 2022. https://www.ymcaworkwell.com/

28 James Clear. *The Goldilocks Rule: How to Stay Motivated in Life and Business.* (Excerpt from *Atomic Habits*). https://jamesclear.com/goldilocks-rule

29 Frances Hutchens. *Stretching: You're Not Tight.* Movementum. 2019. https://movementum.co.uk/journal/2019/5/30/stretching

30   Jason Fox. *How To Lead A Quest: A Guidebook for Pioneering Leaders* (Wiley, 2015).

31   Daniel Kahneman. *Thinking, Fast and Slow* (Anchor Canada, 2013).

32   Joe Alper. *Stretching the Limits.* Science, July 2002, vol 297, issue 5580, 329-331. DOI: 10.1126/science.297.5580.329.

33   Jason Fox. *How To Lead A Quest: A Guidebook for Pioneering Leaders* (Wiley, 2015).

34   Elizabeth Thompson. *Many federal government employees balking at returning to offices.* CBC News. August 2022. https://www.cbc.ca/news/politics/covid-canadian-government-work-1.6543860

35   Keith Ferrazzi, Kian Gohar & Noel Weyrich. *Competing in the New World of Work: How Radical Adaptability Separates the Best from the Rest* (Harvard Business Review Press, 2022): 13.

36   Todd Henry. *Die Empty: Unleash Your Best Work Every Day* (Portfolio, 2015): 18.

37   James Clear. *Atomic Habits: An Easy & Proven Way to Build Good Habits & Break Bad Ones* (Avery, 2018): 38.

38   Julie Fotheringham. Personal Communication. September 2022.

39   As a starting point, check out:
     Barry O'Reilly. *Unlearn: Let Go of Past Success to Achieve Extraordinary Results* (McGraw Hill, 2018).

40   Emily Nagoski & Amelia Nagoski. *Burnout: The Secret to Unlocking the Stress Cycle* (Ballantine Books, 2020).

41   Jennifer Moss. *The Burnout Epidemic: The Rise of Chronic Stress and How We Can Fix It* (Harvard Business Review Press, 2021).

42   YMCA WorkWell. *Insights to Impact: The Depleted, The Overworked and The Underappreciated.* 2021 YMCA WorkWell Workplace Well-Being Report. https://www.ymcaworkwell.com/INSIGHTS-TO-IMPACT-2021

43   David Kaplowitz. *How do you resonate? The importance of energy in leadership.* Rock Spring Coaching. https://www.rockspringcoaching.com/blog1/how-do-you-resonate-the-importance-of-energy-in-leadership

44   Kate Bowler. *No Cure for Being Human (And Other Truths I Need to Hear)* (Random House, 2021).

45   Rob Cross, Wayne Baker & Andrew Parker. *What creates energy in organizations?.* MIT Sloan Management Review. 2003. 44 (4): 51-56. https://sloanreview.mit.edu/article/what-creates-energy-in-organizations

46   Deborah Martin. *What is positive energy and how is it exhibited in the workplace? A qualitative exploration of this elusive concept.* Bucks New University. 4th Applied Positive Psychology Symposium. June 2018. 72-79. http://nectar.northampton.ac.uk/11380/1/2018_APP_Symposium_Proceedings.pdf

47 Kim Cameron. *Practicing Positive Leadership: Tools and Techniques That Create Extraordinary Results* (Berrett-Koehler Publishers, 2013).

48 David Kaplowitz. *How do you resonate? The importance of energy in leadership.* Rock Spring Coaching. https://www.rockspringcoaching.com/blog1/how-do-you-resonate-the-importance-of-energy-in-leadership

49 Jenny Blake. *Free Time: Lose the Busywork, Love Your Business* (Ideapress Publishing, 2022): 95.

50 Kim Cameron. *Positively Energizing Leadership: Virtuous Actions and Relationships That Create High Performance* (Berrett-Koehler Publishers, 2021).

51 Emma Seppälä & Kim Cameron. *The Best Leaders Have a Contagious Positive Energy.* Harvard Business Review. April 2022. https://hbr.org/2022/04/the-best-leaders-have-a-contagious-positive-energy

52 Carolyn Dewar, Scott Keller & Vikram Malhotra. *CEO Excellence: The Six Mindsets That Distinguish the Best Leaders from the Rest* (Scribner, 2022).

53 See also: *9 tips to boost your energy — naturally.* Harvard Health Publishing. August 2020. https://www.health.harvard.edu/energy-and-fatigue/9-tips-to-boost-your-energy-naturally

54 Rob Cross. *Beyond Collaboration Overload: How to Work Smarter, Get Ahead, and Restore Your Well-Being* (Harvard Business Review Press, 2021).

55 Jennifer Moss. *The Burnout Epidemic: The Rise of Chronic Stress and How We Can Fix It* (Harvard Business Review Press, 2021).

56 Neen James. *Folding Time: How to Achieve Twice As Much In Half The Time* (Need James Communications, 2013).

57 Michael D. Watkins. *Harnessing and sustaining energy: the science of good leadership.* I by IMD. September 2021. https://iby.imd.org/leadership/harnessing-and-sustaining-energy-the-science-of-good-leadership/

58 Keith Ferrazzi, Kian Gohar & Noel Weyrich. *Competing in the New World of Work: How Radical Adaptability Separates the Best from the Rest* (Harvard Business Review Press, 2022).

59 Chris Helder. *Useful Belief: Because it's Better than Positive Thinking* (Wiley, 2015).

60 W. Chan Kim & Renee Mauborgne. *Blue Ocean Shift: Beyond Competing - Proven Steps to Inspire Confidence and Seize New Growth* (Hachette Books, 2017).

61 Shane Michael Hatton. *Let's Talk Culture: The conversations you need to create the team you want* (Major Street Publishing, 2022).

62 Jamie Gruman & Deirdre Healey. *Boost: The Science of Recharging Yourself in an Age of Unrelenting Demands* (Information Age Publishing, 2018).

63 Daniel Pink. *When: The Scientific Secrets of Perfect Timing* (Riverhead Books, 2019).

64   Chris McChesney, Sean Covey & Jim Huling. *The 4 Disciplines of Execution: Revised and Updated: Achieving Your Wildly Important Goals* (Simon & Schuster, 2022).

65   Richard Rumelt. *Good Strategy Bad Strategy: The Difference and Why It Matters* (Currency, 2011).

66   Steven D'Souza & Diana Renner. *Not Doing: The Art of Turning Struggle into Ease* (LID Publishing, 2018).

67   Daniel Burrus. *The Anticipatory Organization: Turn Disruption and Change into Opportunity and Advantage* (Greenleaf Book Group Press, 2017).

68   Fuli Li, Tingting Chen, Yun Bai, Robert C. Liden, Man-Nok Wong, and Yan Qiao. *Serving while being energized (strained)? A dual-path model linking servant leadership to leader psychological strain and job performance.* Journal of Applied Psychology September 15, 2022. DOI: 10.1037/apl0001041.

69   Jaquie Scammell. *Service Mindset: 6 mindsets to lead a high-performing service team* (Major Street Publishing, 2020).

70   Kim Cameron. *Positively Energizing Leadership: Virtuous Actions and Relationships That Create High Performance* (Berrett-Koehler Publishers, 2021).

71   Don Miguel Ruiz. *The Four Agreements: A Practical Guide to Personal Freedom* (Amber-Allen Publishing, 1997).

72   Mariam Younan & Kristy A. Martire. *Likeability and Expert Persuasion: Dislikeability Reduces the Perceived Persuasiveness of Expert Evidence.* Frontiers in Psychology. December 2021. DOI: 10.3389/fpsyg.2021.785677.

73   David Ewoldsen & Russell Fazio. *The Accessibility of Source Likability as a Determinant of Persuasion.* Personality and Social Psychology Bulletin. 1992. 18. 19-25. DOI: 10.1177/0146167292181004.

74   Adam Grant. *Give and Take: Why Helping Others Drives Our Success* (Penguin Books, 2014).

75   Eric Barker. *Barking Up the Wrong Tree: The Surprising Science Behind Why Everything You Know About Success Is (Mostly) Wrong* (HarperOne, 2017).

76   Robert Axelrod, quoted in: Eric Barker. *Barking Up the Wrong Tree: The Surprising Science Behind Why Everything You Know About Success Is (Mostly) Wrong* (HarperOne, 2017): 38.

77   Richard Wiseman. *59 Seconds: Think a Little, Change a Lot* (Knopf, 2009).

78   Tom Peters. *The Brand You 50 (Reinventing Work): Fifty Ways to Transform Yourself from an 'Employee' into a Brand That Shouts Distinction, Commitment, and Passion!* (Knopf, 1999).

79   Erin Eatough. *Building influence at work: be the best leader you can be.* BetterUp. July 2021. https://www.betterup.com/blog/building-influence

80   See also: Liz Wiseman. *Impact Players: How to Take the Lead, Play Bigger, and Multiply Your Impact* (Harper Business, 2021).

81 See also: Keith Ferrazzi. *Leading Without Authority: How the New Power of Co-Elevation Can Break Down Silos, Transform Teams, and Reinvent Collaboration* (Currency, 2020).

82 Kieran Flanagan & Dan Gregory. *Forever Skills: The 12 Skills to Futureproof Yourself, Your Team and Your Kids* (Wiley, 2019): 83.

83 Alicia Menendez. *The Likeability Trap: How to Break Free and Succeed as You Are.* (Harper Business, 2019).

84 Hamilton Helmer. *7 Powers: The Foundations of Business Strategy* (Deep Strategy, 2016).

85 Tomas Chamorro-Premuzic. *Forget being nice at work and do these 5 science-backed things instead.* Fast Company. August 2022. https://www.fastcompany.com/90777159/forget-being-nice-at-work-do-this-instead

86 Teresa Amabile. *Brilliant but cruel: Perceptions of negative evaluator.* Journal of Experimental Social Psychology. March 1992. 19 (2): 146-156. DOI: 10.1016/0022-1031(83)90034-3.

87 Eric Barker. *Barking Up the Wrong Tree: The Surprising Science Behind Why Everything You Know About Success Is (Mostly) Wrong* (HarperOne, 2017).

88 Stephen Reysen. *Likability Scale.* https://sites.google.com/site/stephenreysen/psychology-scales/likability-scale (Excerpt from *Construction of a new scale: The Reysen Likability Scale.* Social Behavior and Personality, 33(2): 201-208.DOI: 10.2224/SBP.2005.33.2.201.

89 Nancy MacKay & Alan Weiss. *The Modern Trusted Advisor: Best Practices for High Value Executive Consultation* (Business Expert Press, 2021).

90 Stephen Reysen. *Likability Scale.* https://sites.google.com/site/stephenreysen/psychology-scales/likability-scale (Excerpt from *Construction of a new scale: The Reysen Likability Scale.* Social Behavior and Personality, 33(2): 201-208.DOI: 10.2224/SBP.2005.33.2.201.

91 Likable Person Test. IDRlabs. https://www.idrlabs.com/likable-person/test.php

92 Eric Barker. *Barking Up the Wrong Tree: The Surprising Science Behind Why Everything You Know About Success Is (Mostly) Wrong* (HarperOne, 2017).

93 J.D. Kudisch, M.L Poteet, G.H. Dobbins et al. *Expert power, referent power, and charisma: Toward the resolution of a theoretical debate.* Journal of Business & Psychology. 10, 177–195 (1995). DOI: 10.1007/BF02249578.

94 *What is Referent Power?* The Centre for Leadership Studies. https://situational.com/blog/what-is-referent-power/

95 Abraham Issac, Timothy Bednall, Rupashree Baral, Pierpaolo Magliocca & Amandeo Dhir. *The Effects of Expert and Referent Power on Knowledge Sharing and Hiding.* Journal of Knowledge Management. February 2022. DOI:10.1108/JKM-10-2021-0750.

96 Bernard Marr. *12 Timeless Habits of Likeable Leaders*. https://bernardmarr. com/12-timeless-habits-of-likeable-leaders/

97 Michael Port. *Book Yourself Solid: The Fastest, Easiest, and Most Reliable System for Getting More Clients Than You Can Handle Even if You Hate Marketing and Selling* (Wiley, 2017).

98 Travis Bradberry. *10 Habits of Ultra-Likeable Leaders*. TalentSmart. October 2015. https://www.talentsmarteq.com/articles/10-Habits-of-Ultra-Likeable-Leaders-2147446623-p-1.html/

99 Tomas Chamorro-Premuzic. *Forget being nice at work and do these 5 science-backed things instead*. Fast Company. August 2022. https://www.fastcompany. com/90777159/forget-being-nice-at-work-do-this-instead

100 See also: Robert Hogan & Dana Shelton. *A Socioanalytic Perspective on Job Performance*. Human Performance. 1998. 11(2-3): 129-144, DOI: 10.1080/08959285.1998.9668028.

101 Travis Bradberry. *10 Habits of Ultra-Likeable Leaders*. TalentSmart. October 2015. https://www.talentsmarteq.com/articles/10-Habits-of-Ultra-Likeable-Leaders-2147446623-p-1.html/

102 Chris Voss. *Never Split the Difference: Negotiating as if Your Life Depended on It* (Random House, 2017).

103 The Leadership Institute. *27 Secrets of Likeable Leaders*. December 2019. https://www.theleadershipinstitute.com.au/2019/12/ the-27-secrets-of-likeable-leaders/

104 Carey Nieuwhof. *3 Hard But Powerful Truths about Likeability and Leadership*. https://careynieuwhof.com/3-hard-powerful-truths-likeability-leadership/

105 Jenn Lofgren. *Being A Likeable Leader Doesn't Mean Being Liked All The Time*. Forbes. October 2021. https://www. forbes.com/sites/forbescoachescouncil/2021/10/18/ being-a-likeable-leader-doesnt-mean-being-liked-all-the-time/

106 *What is Referent Power?* The Centre for Leadership Studies. https://situational. com/blog/what-is-referent-power/

107 Maggie Wooll. *What is referent power? Your guide as a leader*. BetterUp. November 2021. https://www.betterup.com/blog/what-is-referent-power

108 Ken Gosnell. *How To Become A Likable Leader*. Forbes. October 2018. https://www.forbes.com/sites/forbescoachescouncil/2018/10/12/ how-to-become-a-likable-leader/

109 Jim Collins. *Level 5 Leadership* (Excerpt from *Good to Great*). https://www. jimcollins.com/concepts/level-five-leadership.html

110 Vanessa Bohns. *You Have More Influence Than You Think: How We Underestimate Our Powers of Persuasion, and Why It Matters* (WW Norton, 2021).

111 My current favourite go-to for learning team interpersonal skills is Chad Littlefield at weand.me

112 Adam Grant. *Think Again: The Power of Knowing What You Don't Know* (Viking, 2021).

113 Heather McGowan & Chris Shipley. *The Adaptation Advantage: Let Go, Learn Fast, and Thrive in the Future of Work* (Wiley, 2020).

114 April Rinne. *Flux: 8 Superpowers for Thriving in Constant Change* (Berrett-Koehler Publishers, 2021).

115 *Author Talks: April Rinne on finding calm and meaning in a world of flux.* McKinsey & Company. August 2021. https://www.mckinsey.com/featured-insights/mckinsey-on-books/author-talks-april-rinne-on-finding-calm-and-meaning-in-a-world-of-flux

116 Natalie Fratto. *3 ways to measure your adaptability — and how to improve it.* TED Talk. 2019. https://www.ted.com/talks/natalie_fratto_3_ways_to_measure_your_adaptability_and_how_to_improve_it

117 The concept of "bounce" as an ability to move forward fast and grow out of adversity is identified as a growing contributor to resilience in the *2022 Global Resilience Report.* The Resilience Institute. 2022. https://resiliencei.com/resilience-research/2022-report/

118 Keith Ferrazzi, Kian Gohar & Noel Weyrich. *Competing in the New World of Work: How Radical Adaptability Separates the Best from the Rest* (Harvard Business Review Press, 2022).

119 McKinsey & Company. *Future proof: Solving the 'adaptability paradox' for the long term.* August 2021. https://www.mckinsey.com/business-functions/people-and-organizational-performance/our-insights/future-proof-solving-the-adaptability-paradox-for-the-long-term

120 Julian Birkinshaw and Cristina Gibson. *Building Ambidexterity Into an Organization.* MIT Sloan Management Review. 2004. 45(4): 47. https://sloan-review.mit.edu/article/building-ambidexterity-into-an-organization/

121 McKinsey & Company. *Future proof: Solving the 'adaptability paradox' for the long term.* August 2021. https://www.mckinsey.com/business-functions/people-and-organizational-performance/our-insights/future-proof-solving-the-adaptability-paradox-for-the-long-term

122 Mary Uhl-Bien & Michael Arena. *Leadership for organizational adaptability: A theoretical synthesis and integrative framework.* The Leadership Quarterly. January 2018. 29 (1): 89-104. DOI: 10.1016/j.leaqua.2017.12.009.

123 Kelly McGonigal. *The Willpower Instinct: How Self-Control Works, Why It Matters, and What You Can Do to Get More of It* (Avery, 2013).

124 See for example:

McKinsey & Company. *Defining the skills citizens will need in the future world of work.* June 2021. https://www.ic3institute.org/resourcelibrary/wp-content/uploads/2022/03/defining-the-skills-citizens-will-need-in-the-future-of-work-final.pdf

Jessica Schueller & Hugo Figueiredo. *Adaptability is set to be the key skill for the future.* University World News. July 2021. https://www.universityworldnews.com/post.php?story=20210702110012289

125 McKinsey & Company. *Future proof: Solving the 'adaptability paradox' for the long term.* August 2021. https://www.mckinsey.com/business-functions/people-and-organizational-performance/our-insights/future-proof-solving-the-adaptability-paradox-for-the-long-term

126 *Author Talks: April Rinne on finding calm and meaning in a world of flux.* McKinsey & Company. August 2021.

127 McKinsey & Company. *Future proof: Solving the 'adaptability paradox' for the long term.* August 2021. https://www.mckinsey.com/business-functions/people-and-organizational-performance/our-insights/future-proof-solving-the-adaptability-paradox-for-the-long-term

128 Carolyn Dewar, Scott Keller & Vikram Malhotra. CEO Excellence: The Six Mindsets That Distinguish the Best Leaders from the Rest (Scribner, 2022).

129 Julian Birkinshaw and Cristina Gibson. *Building Ambidexterity Into an Organization.* MIT Sloan Management Review. 2004. 45(4): 47. https://sloanreview.mit.edu/article/building-ambidexterity-into-an-organization/

130 AQai. https://www.aqai.io/

131 AQai. https://www.aqai.io/

132 Golnaz Tabibnia & Dan Radecki. *Resilience training that can change the brain.* Consulting Psychology Journal: Practice and Research. 2018. 70 (1):59-88. DOI: 10.1037/cpb0000110.

133 *Author Talks: April Rinne on finding calm and meaning in a world of flux.* McKinsey & Company. August 2021.

134 McKinsey & Company. *Future proof: Solving the 'adaptability paradox' for the long term.* August 2021. https://www.mckinsey.com/business-functions/people-and-organizational-performance/our-insights/future-proof-solving-the-adaptability-paradox-for-the-long-term

135 McKinsey & Company. *Future proof: Solving the 'adaptability paradox' for the long term.* August 2021. https://www.mckinsey.com/business-functions/people-and-organizational-performance/our-insights/future-proof-solving-the-adaptability-paradox-for-the-long-term

136 Kiddy & Partners. *Why adaptability is a critical capability for future leadership.* Gateley. November 2020. https://gateleyplc.com/insight/quick-reads/why-adaptability-is-a-critical-capability-for-future-leadership/

137 Monica Thakrar. *How To Become An Adaptable Leader.* Forbes. January 2020. https://www.forbes.com/sites/forbescoachescouncil/2020/01/16/how-to-become-an-adaptable-leader/?sh=48d682e014b6

138 McKinsey & Company. *Future proof: Solving the 'adaptability paradox' for the long term.* August 2021. https://www.mckinsey.com/business-functions/people-and-organizational-performance/our-insights/future-proof-solving-the-adaptability-paradox-for-the-long-term

139 Golnaz Tabibnia & Dan Radecki. *Resilience training that can change the brain.* Consulting Psychology Journal: Practice and Research. 2018. 70 (1):59-88. DOI: 10.1037/cpb0000110.

140 Todd Henry. *Die Empty: Unleash Your Best Work Every Day* (Portfolio, 2015): 130.

141 Heather McGowan & Chris Shipley. *The Adaptation Advantage: Let Go, Learn Fast, and Thrive in the Future of Work* (Wiley, 2020).

142 Kelly McGonigal. *The Willpower Instinct: How Self-Control Works, Why It Matters, and What You Can Do to Get More of It* (Avery, 2013).

143 Benjamin Hardy. *Be Your Future Self Now: The Science of Intentional Transformation* (Hay House Business, 2022): 9.

144 Kieran Flanagan & Dan Gregory. *Forever Skills: The 12 Skills to Futureproof Yourself, Your Team and Your Kids* (Wiley, 2019).

145 AQai. https://www.aqai.io/

146 Allan Calarco. *Adaptable Leadership: What It Takes to Be a Quick-Change Artist.* Center for Creative Leadership. 2020. https://www.ccl.org/articles/white-papers/adaptable-leadership/

147 Keith Ferrazzi, Kian Gohar & Noel Weyrich. *Competing in the New World of Work: How Radical Adaptability Separates the Best from the Rest* (Harvard Business Review Press, 2022): 215.

148 McKinsey & Company. *Future proof: Solving the 'adaptability paradox' for the long term.* August 2021. https://www.mckinsey.com/business-functions/people-and-organizational-performance/our-insights/future-proof-solving-the-adaptability-paradox-for-the-long-term

149 *2021 Workplace Learning Report.* LinkedIn Learning. https://learning.linkedin.com/resources/workplace-learning-report-2021

150 McKinsey & Company. *Future proof: Solving the 'adaptability paradox' for the long term.* August 2021. https://www.mckinsey.com/business-functions/people-and-organizational-performance/our-insights/future-proof-solving-the-adaptability-paradox-for-the-long-term

151 Kiddy & Partners. *Why adaptability is a critical capability for future leadership.* Gateley. November 2020. https://gateleyplc.com/insight/quick-reads/why-adaptability-is-a-critical-capability-for-future-leadership/

152 Barry O'Reilly. *Unlearn: Let Go of Past Success to Achieve Extraordinary Results* (McGraw Hill, 2018).

153 Gary Hamel & Bill Breen. *The Future of Management* (Harvard Business Review Press, 2007).

154 Mary Uhl-Bien & Michael Arena. *Leadership for organizational adaptability: A theoretical synthesis and integrative framework*. The Leadership Quarterly. January 2018. 29 (1): 89-104. DOI: 10.1016/j.leaqua.2017.12.009.

155 Mary Uhl-Bien & Michael Arena. *Leadership for organizational adaptability: A theoretical synthesis and integrative framework*. The Leadership Quarterly. January 2018. 29 (1): 89-104. DOI: 10.1016/j.leaqua.2017.12.009.

156 Edgar H. Schein. *Humble Consulting: How to Provide Real Help Faster* (Berrett-Koehler Publishers, 2016).

157 Ryan Holiday. *The Obstacle Is the Way: The Timeless Art of Turning Trials into Triumph* (Portfolio, 2014).

158 Natalie Fratto. *3 ways to measure your adaptability — and how to improve it*. TED Talk. 2019.

159 See also: Allan Calarco. *Adaptable Leadership: What It Takes to Be a Quick-Change Artist*. Center for Creative Leadership. 2020. https://www.ccl.org/articles/white-papers/adaptable-leadership/

160 Keith Keating. *3 Traits of Adaptable Leaders*. Association for Talent Development. March 2021. https://www.td.org/insights/3-traits-of-adaptable-leaders

161 Rosie Yeo. *Go for Bold: How to Create Powerful Strategy in Uncertain Times* (Major Street Publishing, 2022): 17.

162 Nilofer Merchant. *The Power of Onlyness: Make Your Wild Ideas Mighty Enough to Dent the World* (Viking, 2017).

163 Jim Collins & Jerry Porras. *Built to Last: Successful Habits of Visionary Companies* (Harper Business; 3rd ed. 2004).

164 Rebecca Sutherns. *Sightline: Strategic plans that gather momentum not dust.* (Hambone Publishing, 2020).

165 Maggie Wooll. *Everything you need to know about strategic leadership*. BetterUp. April 2021. https://www.betterup.com/blog/strategic-leadership

166 Rosie Yeo. *Go for Bold: How to Create Powerful Strategy in Uncertain Times* (Major Street Publishing, 2022).

167 Julie Zhuo. *How to Become a Strategic Leader*. MIT Sloan Management Review. May 2019. https://sloanreview.mit.edu/article/how-to-become-a-strategic-leader/

168 Henry Mintzberg, Joseph Lampel & Bruce Ahlstrand. *Strategy Safari: A Guided Tour Through the Wilds of Strategic Management* (Free Press, 2005).

169 Richard P. Rumelt. *The Crux: How Leaders Become Strategists* (PublicAffairs, 2022): 11.

170 Daniel Burrus. *The Anticipatory Organization: Turn Disruption and Change into Opportunity and Advantage* (Greenleaf Book Group Press, 2017).

171 A.G. Lafley & Roger L. Martin. *Playing to Win: How Strategy Really Works* (Harvard Business Review Press, 2013): 4.

172 Steven D'Souza & Diana Renner. *Not Doing: The Art of Turning Struggle into Ease* (LID Publishing, 2018).

173 Dorie Clark. *The Long Game: How to Be a Long-Term Thinker in a Short-Term World* (Harvard Business Review Press, 2021).

174 Carolyn Dewar, Scott Keller & Vikram Malhotra. *CEO Excellence: The Six Mindsets That Distinguish the Best Leaders from the Rest* (Scribner, 2022).

175 Dorie Clark. *The Long Game: How to Be a Long-Term Thinker in a Short-Term World* (Harvard Business Review Press, 2021).

176 Oliver Burkeman. *Four Thousand Weeks: Time Management for Mortals* (Allen Lane, 2021).

177 adrienne maree brown. *Emergent Strategy: Shaping Change, Changing Worlds* (AK Press, 2017).

178 adrienne maree brown. *Emergent Strategy: Shaping Change, Changing Worlds* (AK Press, 2017).

179 adrienne maree brown. *Holding Change: The Way of Emergent Strategy Facilitation and Mediation* (AK Press, 2021).

180 John M. Bryson. *Strategic Planning for Public and Nonprofit Organizations: A Guide to Strengthening and Sustaining Organizational Achievement* (Wiley, 2018).

181 Rosie Yeo. *Go for Bold: How to Create Powerful Strategy in Uncertain Times* (Major Street Publishing, 2022): 62.

182 A.G. Lafley & Roger L. Martin. *Playing to Win: How Strategy Really Works* (Harvard Business Review Press, 2013): 176.

183 Keith Ferrazzi, Kian Gohar & Noel Weyrich. *Competing in the New World of Work: How Radical Adaptability Separates the Best from the Rest* (Harvard Business Review Press, 2022).

184 David Nour & Lin Wilson. *Curve Benders: How Strategic Relationships Can Power Your Non-linear Growth in the Future of Work* (Wiley, 2021).

185 Jessica Leitch, David Lancefield & Mark Dawson. 10 principles of strategic leadership. PwC. strategy+business. Autumn 2016. Issue 84. https://www.strategy-business.com/article/10-Principles-of-Strategic-Leadership

186 Dorie Clark. *The Long Game: How to Be a Long-Term Thinker in a Short-Term World* (Harvard Business Review Press, 2021).

187 Jenny Blake. *Free Time: Lose the Busywork, Love Your Business* (Ideapress Publishing, 2022): 105.

188 Jessica Leitch, David Lancefield & Mark Dawson. *10 principles of strategic leadership*. PwC. strategy+business. Autumn 2016. Issue 84. https://www.strategy-business.com/article/10-Principles-of-Strategic-Leadership

189 Jessica Leitch, David Lancefield & Mark Dawson. *10 principles of strategic leadership*. PwC. strategy+business. Autumn 2016. Issue 84. https://www.strategy-business.com/article/10-Principles-of-Strategic-Leadership

190 Maggie Wooll. *Everything you need to know about strategic leadership*. BetterUp. April 2021. https://www.betterup.com/blog/strategic-leadership

191 *6 Skills You Need to Become A Strategic Leader*. The Strategy Institute. June 2021. https://www.thestrategyinstitute.org/insights/6-skills-you-need-to-become-a-strategic-leader

192 Dorie Clark. *The Long Game: How to Be a Long-Term Thinker in a Short-Term World* (Harvard Business Review Press, 2021).

193 For more information see: Shane Michael Hatton. *Let's Talk Culture: The conversations you need to create the team you want* (Major Street Publishing, 2022).

194 Rosie Yeo. *Go for Bold: How to Create Powerful Strategy in Uncertain Times* (Major Street Publishing, 2022).

195 Dorie Clark. *The Long Game: How to Be a Long-Term Thinker in a Short-Term World* (Harvard Business Review Press, 2021).

196 Simon Sinek. *Leaders Eat Last: Why Some Teams Pull Together and Others Don't* (Portfolio, 2017).

197 Amy Cuddy. *Presence: Bringing Your Boldest Self to Your Biggest Challenges* (Little, Brown Spark, 2018).

198 Joel Brockner. *The Process Matters: Engaging and Equipping People for Success* (Princeton University Press, 2017).

199 Kurt T. Dirks. *Trust in leadership and team performance: Evidence from NCAA basketball*. Journal of Applied Psychology, 2000, 86(6): 1004-1012. DOI: 10.1037//0021-9010.85.6.1004.

200 Eric Barker. *Barking Up the Wrong Tree: The Surprising Science Behind Why Everything You Know About Success Is (Mostly) Wrong* (HarperOne, 2017).

201 Abbey Lewis. *Good Leadership? It All Starts With Trust*. Harvard Business Learning. 2021. https://www.harvardbusiness.org/good-leadership-it-all-starts-with-trust/

202 Tom Rath Barry Conchie. *Strengths Based Leadership: Great Leaders, Teams, and Why People Follow* (Gallup Press, 2009).

203 Simon Sinek. *The Infinite Game* (Portfolio, 2019).

204 See for example: David Maister, Charles H. Green & Robert M. Galford. *The Trusted Advisor* (Free Press, 2001).

205 adrienne maree brown. *trust the people.* 2019. https://adriennemareebrown.net/2019/07/01/trust-the-people-2/

206 Stephen M.R. Covey & Greg Link. *Smart Trust: Creating Prosperity, Energy, and Joy in a Low-Trust World* (Free Press, 2012).

207 Stephen M.R. Covey. *Trust and Inspire: How Truly Great Leaders Unleash Greatness in Others* (Simon & Schuster, 2022): 130.

208 Stephen M.R. Covey. *Trust and Inspire: How Truly Great Leaders Unleash Greatness in Others* (Simon & Schuster, 2022).

209 Marcus Buckingham. *Love and Work: How to Find What You Love, Love What You Do, and Do It for the Rest of Your Life* (Harvard Business Review Press, 2022).

210 Eric Barker. *Barking Up the Wrong Tree: The Surprising Science Behind Why Everything You Know About Success Is (Mostly) Wrong* (HarperOne, 2017).

211 David Maister, Charles H. Green & Robert M. Galford. *The Trusted Advisor* (Free Press, 2001).

212 David Maister, Charles H. Green & Robert M. Galford. *The Trusted Advisor* (Free Press, 2001).

213 Yuan, quoted in: Stephen M.R. Covey. *Trust and Inspire: How Truly Great Leaders Unleash Greatness in Others* (Simon & Schuster, 2022).

214 See also: Stephen M.R. Covey. *The Speed of Trust* (Free Press, 2008).

215 Adam Kahane. *Collaborating with the Enemy: How to Work with People You Don't Agree with or Like or Trust* (Berrett-Koehler Publishers, 2017).

216 Walter Wangerin Jr. *As For Me and My House: Crafting Your Marriage to Last* (Thomas Nelson, 2001).

217 Brené Brown. *Daring Greatly: How the Courage to Be Vulnerable Transforms the Way We Live, Love, Parent, and Lead* (Avery, 2015).

218 Brené Brown. *Dare to Lead: Brave Work. Tough Conversations. Whole Hearts.* (Random House, 2018).

219 Kieran Flanagan & Dan Gregory. *Forever Skills: The 12 Skills to Futureproof Yourself, Your Team and Your Kids* (Wiley, 2019).

220 Eagle's Flight. https://www.eaglesflight.com/

221 Chris Voss. *Never Split the Difference: Negotiating as if Your Life Depended on It* (Random House, 2017).

222 Eric Barker. *Barking Up the Wrong Tree: The Surprising Science Behind Why Everything You Know About Success Is (Mostly) Wrong* (HarperOne, 2017).

223 Edgar Schein & Peter Schein. *Humble Inquiry, Second Edition: The Gentle Art of Asking Instead of Telling* (Berrett-Koehler Publishers, 2021).

224 David Grossman. *Trust in the Workplace: 10 Steps to Build Trust with Employees.* Leader Communicator Blog. June 2022. https://www.yourthoughtpartner.com/blog/bid/59619/leaders-follow-these-6-steps-to-build-trust-with-employees-improve-how-you-re-perceived

225 David Maister, Charles H. Green & Robert M. Galford. *The Trusted Advisor* (Free Press, 2001).

226 Joel Brockner. *The Process Matters: Engaging and Equipping People for Success* (Princeton University Press, 2017).

227 Centre for Creative Leadership. *Why Leadership Trust Is Critical in Times of Change and Disruption.* June 2022. https://www.ccl.org/articles/leading-effectively-articles/why-leadership-trust-is-critical-in-times-of-change-and-disruption/

228 Rosie Yeo. *Go for Bold: How to Create Powerful Strategy in Uncertain Times* (Major Street Publishing, 2022).

229 Kenneth Cukier, Viktor Mayer-Schönberger & Francis de Véricourt. *Framers: Human Advantage in an Age of Technology and Turmoil* (Dutton, 2021).

230 Some recent exceptions from which I will draw on frequently in this section: Martin Reeves & Jack Fuller. *The Imagination Machine: How to Spark New Ideas and Create Your Company's Future* (Harvard Business Review Press, 2021).

Rob Hopkins. *From What Is to What If: Unleashing the Power of Imagination to Create the Future We Want* (Chelsea Green Publishing, 2019).

231 Martin Reeves & Jack Fuller. *The Imagination Machine: How to Spark New Ideas and Create Your Company's Future* (Harvard Business Review Press, 2021): 10.

232 Gerardo Patriotta. *Imagination, Self-Knowledge, and Poise: Jim March's Lessons for Leadership.* Journal of Management Studies. October 2019. 56(8). DOI:10.1111/joms.12536.

233 Eric Weiner. *The Geography of Genius: A Search for the World's Most Creative Places from Ancient Athens to Silicon Valley* (Simon & Schuster, 2016).

234 Linda Hill, Greg Brandeau, Emily Truelove & Kent Lineback. *Collective Genius: The Art and Practice of Leading Innovation* (Harvard Business Review Press, 2014).

235 Eric Liu & Scott Noppe-Brandon. *Imagination First: Unlocking the Power of Possibility* (Jossey-Bass, 2011).

236 Jenny Blake. *Free Time: Lose the Busywork, Love Your Business* (Ideapress Publishing, 2022).

237 John Pollack. *Shortcut: How Analogies Reveal Connections, Spark Innovation, and Sell Our Greatest Ideas* (Avery, 2015).

238 Kelli R. Pearson. *Imaginative Leadership: A Conceptual Frame for the Design and Facilitation of Creative Methods and Generative Engagement.* From the book *Co-Creativity and Engaged Scholarship*: 176. January 2022. DOI:10.1007/978-3-030-84248-2_6.

239 Gillian Judson. *Cultivating Leadership Imagination with Cognitive Tools: An Imagination-Focused Approach to Leadership Education.* Journal of Research on Leadership Education. June 2021. DOI: 10.1177/19427751211022028.

240 Jason Fox. *How To Lead A Quest: A Guidebook for Pioneering Leaders* (Wiley, 2015).

241 Gerardo Patriotta. *Imagination, Self-Knowledge, and Poise: Jim March's Lessons for Leadership.* Journal of Management Studies. October 2019. 56(8). DOI:10.1111/joms.12536.

242 Benjamin Hardy. *Be Your Future Self Now: The Science of Intentional Transformation* (Hay House Business, 2022): 79.

243 Oliver Burkeman. *Four Thousand Weeks: Time Management for Mortals* (Allen Lane, 2021): 4.

244 Ross Thornley. *The Importance of Context: Why We Need To Think Collaboratively If We Are To Adapt.* Medium. February 2020. https://medium.com/@rossthornley/the-importance-of-context-why-we-need-to-think-collaboratively-if-we-are-to-adapt-1dba937003a8

245 Brian Paradis. *Lead with Imagination* (Forefront Books, 2019).

246 *From What Is to What If: Unleashing the Power of Imagination to Create the Future We Want* (Chelsea Green Publishing, 2019).

247 Charles Duhigg. *Smarter Faster Better: The Transformative Power of Real Productivity* (Anchor Canada, 2017).

248 See also: Kenneth Cukier, Viktor Mayer-Schönberger & Francis de Véricourt. *Framers: Human Advantage in an Age of Technology and Turmoil* (Dutton, 2021).

249 Margaret Heffernan. *Uncharted: How to Navigate the Future* (Avid Reader Press / Simon & Schuster, 2020).

250 Gillian Judson. *Cultivating Leadership Imagination with Cognitive Tools: An Imagination-Focused Approach to Leadership Education.* Journal of Research on Leadership Education. June 2021. DOI: 10.1177/19427751211022028.

251 Martin Reeves & Jack Fuller. *The Imagination Machine: How to Spark New Ideas and Create Your Company's Future* (Harvard Business Review Press, 2021).

252 Leadership Now. *7 Principles to Lead with Imagination.* June 2019. https://www.leadershipnow.com/leadingblog/2019/06/7_principles_to_lead_with_imag.html

253 Kendra Sand. *How to Expand Your Imagination in 8 Days.* TEDxMIleHigh. October 2019. https://www.tedxmilehigh.com/how-expand-imagination/

254 Margaret Heffernan. *Uncharted: How to Navigate the Future* (Avid Reader Press / Simon & Schuster, 2020).

255 Gillian Judson. *Cultivating Leadership Imagination with Cognitive Tools: An Imagination-Focused Approach to Leadership Education.* Journal of Research on Leadership Education. June 2021. DOI: 10.1177/19427751211022028.

256 Kendra Sand. *How to Expand Your Imagination in 8 Days.* TEDxMIleHigh. October 2019. https://www.tedxmilehigh.com/how-expand-imagination/

257 Margaret Heffernan. *Uncharted: How to Navigate the Future* (Avid Reader Press / Simon & Schuster, 2020): 59.

258 Kenneth Cukier, Viktor Mayer-Schönberger & Francis de Véricourt. *Framers: Human Advantage in an Age of Technology and Turmoil* (Dutton, 2021): 101.

259 Martin Reeves & Jack Fuller. *The Imagination Machine: How to Spark New Ideas and Create Your Company's Future* (Harvard Business Review Press, 2021).

260 Martin Reeves & Jack Fuller. *The Imagination Machine: How to Spark New Ideas and Create Your Company's Future* (Harvard Business Review Press, 2021).

261 Pete Davis. *Dedicated: The Case for Commitment in an Age of Infinite Browsing* (Avid Reader Press / Simon & Schuster, 2021): 238.

262 adrienne maree brown. *Holding Change: The Way of Emergent Strategy Facilitation and Mediation* (AK Press, 2021).

263 Charles D. Spielberger & Eric C. Reheiser. *Assessment of Emotions: Anxiety, Anger, Depression, and Curiosity.* Applied Psychology: Health and Well-Being. September 2009, 1(3): 271-302. DOI: 10.1111/j.1758-0854.2009.01017.x.

264 Todd Henry. *Die Empty: Unleash Your Best Work Every Day* (Portfolio, 2015).

265 Diane Hamilton. *Cracking the Curiosity Code: The Key to Unlocking Human Potential* (Dr. Diane Hamilton LLC, 2019).

266 Merck. *Our State of Curiosity.* https://www.emdgroup.com/en/company/curiosity/our-curiosity.html

267 Todd B. Kashdan. *What Are the Five Dimensions of Curiosity?* Psychology Today. January 2018. https://www.psychologytoday.com/ca/blog/curious/201801/what-are-the-five-dimensions-curiosity

268 Merck. *2020 State of Curiosity Report.* https://www.emdgroup.com/company/us/State-of-Curiosity-Report-2020-US.pdf

269 See also: Todd B. Kashdan, Fallon R. Goodman, David J. Disabato, Patrick E. McKnight, Kerry Kelso &Carl Naughton. *Curiosity has comprehensive benefits in the workplace: Developing and validating a multidimensional workplace curiosity scale in United States and German employees.* Personality and Individual Differences. 2020, 155. Volume 155, 109717. DOI: 10.1016/j.paid.2019.109717.

270 This is a student exchange program.

271 *The Curiosity Index: Ranking Europe's Most Curious Nations.* The Viking Blog. May 2019. https://blog.viking-direct.co.uk/ curiosity-index-ranking-europes-curious-nations

272 Edgar Schein & Peter Schein. *Humble Inquiry, Second Edition: The Gentle Art of Asking Instead of Telling* (Berrett-Koehler Publishers, 2021).

273 Merck. *2020 State of Curiosity Report.* https://www.emdgroup.com/company/ us/State-of-Curiosity-Report-2020-US.pdf

274 Ian Leslie. *Curious: The Desire to Know and Why Your Future Depends on It* (Basic Books, 2015).

275 Peter H. Diamandis & Steven Kotler. *The Future Is Faster Than You Think: How Converging Technologies Are Transforming Business, Industries, and Our Lives* (Simon & Schuster, 2020).

276 Shirzad Chamine. *Positive Intelligence: Positive Intelligence: Why Only 20% of Teams and Individuals Achieve Their True Potential and How You Can Achieve Yours* (Greenleaf Book Group Press, 2012).

277 James Clear. *Atomic Habits: An Easy & Proven Way to Build Good Habits & Break Bad Ones* (Avery, 2018): 261.

278 Diane Hamilton. *Cracking the Curiosity Code: The Key to Unlocking Human Potential* (Dr. Diane Hamilton LLC, 2019): 64.

279 C. Kidd & B. Y. Hayden. *The Psychology and Neuroscience of Curiosity.* Neuron. 2015 Nov 4;88(3):449-60. DOI: 10.1016/j.neuron.2015.09.010.

280 Edgar Schein & Peter Schein. *Humble Inquiry, Second Edition: The Gentle Art of Asking Instead of Telling* (Berrett-Koehler Publishers, 2021).

281 Jennifer Moss. *The Burnout Epidemic: The Rise of Chronic Stress and How We Can Fix It* (Harvard Business Review Press, 2021).

282 Alexandra Drake, Bruce P. Doré, Emily B. Falk, Perry Zurn, Danielle S. Bassett & David M. Lydon-Staley. *Daily Stressor-Related Negative Mood and its Associations with Flourishing and Daily Curiosity.* Journal of Happiness Studies. 2022. Volume 23: 423-438. DOI: 10.1007/s10902-021-00404-2.

283 Martin Reeves & Jack Fuller. *The Imagination Machine: How to Spark New Ideas and Create Your Company's Future* (Harvard Business Review Press, 2021).

284 Todd Henry. *Die Empty: Unleash Your Best Work Every Day* (Portfolio, 2015).

285 Dan Heath. *Upstream: The Quest to Solve Problems Before They Happen* (Avid Reader Press /Simon & Schuster, 2020).

286 Lydia Paine Hagtvedt, Karyn Dossinger, Spencer H. Harrison & Li Huang. *Curiosity made the cat more creative: Specific curiosity as a driver of creativity.* Organizational Behavior and Human Decision Processes. 2019, Volume 150: 1-13. DOI: 10.1016/j.obhdp.2018.10.007.

287 Gary Klein. *Seeing What Others Don't: The Remarkable Ways We Gain Insights* (Public Affairs, 2015).

288 Rob Urbach. *Why Curiosity is an Essential Leadership Trait.* Thrive. https://thrive-global.com/stories/why-curiosity-is-an-essential-leadership-trait/

289 Amanda Lang. *The Power Of Why* (Collins Canada, 2012).

290 McKinsey & Company. *Defining the skills citizens will need in the future world of work.* June 2021. https://www.ic3institute.org/resourcelibrary/wp-content/uploads/2022/03/defining-the-skills-citizens-will-need-in-the-future-of-work-final.pdf

291 Amanda Lang. *The Power Of Why* (Collins Canada, 2012).

292 Veljko Jovanovic & Dragana Brdaric. *Did curiosity kill the cat? Evidence from subjective well-being in adolescents.* Personality and Individual Differences. 2012, 52(3): 380-384. DOI: 10.1016/j.paid.2011.10.043.

293 Jay Steven Levin. *Curiosity: The Leadership Killer You Won't See Coming.* Forbes. June 2021. https://www.forbes.com/sites/forbescoachescouncil/2021/06/01/lack-of-curiosity-killed-the-leader/

294 Alexandra Drake, Bruce P. Doré, Emily B. Falk, Perry Zurn, Danielle S. Bassett & David M. Lydon-Staley. *Daily Stressor-Related Negative Mood and its Associations with Flourishing and Daily Curiosity.* Journal of Happiness Studies. 2022. Volume 23: 423-438. DOI: 10.1007/s10902-021-00404-2.

295 Diane Hamilton. *Cracking the Curiosity Code: The Key to Unlocking Human Potential* (Dr. Diane Hamilton LLC, 2019).

296 Alexandra Drake, Bruce P. Doré, Emily B. Falk, Perry Zurn, Danielle S. Bassett & David M. Lydon-Staley. *Daily Stressor-Related Negative Mood and its Associations with Flourishing and Daily Curiosity.* Journal of Happiness Studies. 2022. Volume 23: 423-438. DOI: 10.1007/s10902-021-00404-2.

297 See also: Georgia Murch. *Fixing Feedback* (Wiley, 2016).

298 Marcus Buckingham. *Love and Work: How to Find What You Love, Love What You Do, and Do It for the Rest of Your Life* (Harvard Business Review Press, 2022).

299 Francesca Gino. *The Business Case for Curiosity.* Harvard Business Review. 2018. https://hbr.org/2018/09/the-business-case-for-curiosity

300 Rob Urbach. Why Curiosity is an Essential Leadership Trait. Thrive. https://thriveglobal.com/stories/why-curiosity-is-an-essential-leadership-trait/

301 Shirzad Chamine. *Positive Intelligence: Positive Intelligence: Why Only 20% of Teams and Individuals Achieve Their True Potential and How You Can Achieve Yours* (Greenleaf Book Group Press, 2012).

302 Dorie Clark. The Long Game: How to Be a Long-Term Thinker in a Short-Term World (Harvard Business Review Press, 2021).

303 Maile Toplif. *Curiosity and Leadership.* Realizing Leadership. 2013, 9: 18-23. http://mailetopliff.com/mtimain/wp-content/uploads/2019/03/CuriosityandLeadership.pdf

304 Diane Hamilton. *Innovative Leadership: Developing Curiosity.* Future Learn. https://www.futurelearn.com/courses/developing-curiosity

305 Stephynie Malik. *Curiosity: A Leadership Trait That Can Transform Your Business To Achieve Extraordinary Results.* Forbes. 2020. https://www.forbes.com/sites/forbescoachescouncil/2020/08/26/curiosity-a-leadership-trait-that-can-transform-your-business-to-achieve-extraordinary-results

306 Jay Steven Levin. *Curiosity: The Leadership Killer You Won't See Coming.* Forbes. 2021. https://www.forbes.com/sites/forbescoachescouncil/2021/06/01/lack-of-curiosity-killed-the-leader

307 Alison Horstmeyer. *The generative role of curiosity in soft skills development for contemporary VUCA environments.* Journal of Organizational Change Management. 2020, 33(5): 737-751. DOI: 10.1108/JOCM-08-2019-0250.

308 Paul Ashcroft, Simon Brown & Garrick Jones. *The Curious Advantage* (Laiki Publishing, 2020): 68.

309 Daniel H. Pink. *Drive: The Surprising Truth About What Motivates Us* (Riverhead Books, 2011).

310 John C. Maxwell. *Beyond Talent: Become Someone Who Gets Extraordinary Results* (Harper Collins Leadership, 2011).

311 Stuart Firestein. *The Pursuit of Ignorance.* TED2013. https://www.ted.com/talks/stuart_firestein_the_pursuit_of_ignorance

312 Adam Grant. *Think Again: The Power of Knowing What You Don't Know* (Viking, 2021).

313 Yuval Noah Harari. *21 Lessons for the 21st Century* (Signal, 2020).

314 Diane Hamilton. *Innovative Leadership: Developing Curiosity.* Future Learn. https://www.futurelearn.com/courses/developing-curiosity

315 Francesca Gino. *The Business Case for Curiosity.* Harvard Business Review. 2018. https://hbr.org/2018/09/the-business-case-for-curiosity

316 Francesca Gino. *The Business Case for Curiosity.* Harvard Business Review. 2018. https://hbr.org/2018/09/the-business-case-for-curiosity

317 Lieke L. F. van Lieshout, Floris P. de Lange & Roshan Cools. *Uncertainty increases curiosity, but decreases happiness.* Scientific Reports. 2021. DOI: 10.1038/s41598-021-93464-6.

318 Kathy Taberner and Kirsten Taberner Siggins. *The Power of Curiosity: How to Have Real Conversations That Create Collaboration, Innovation and Understanding* (Morgan James Publishing, 2015).

319 Julia Galef. *The Scout Mindset: Why Some People See Things Clearly and Others Don't* (Penguin Publishing Group, 2021).

320 adrienne maree brown. *Holding Change: The Way of Emergent Strategy Facilitation and Mediation* (AK Press, 2021): 113.

321 Francesca Gino. *The Business Case for Curiosity.* Harvard Business Review. 2018. https://hbr.org/2018/09/the-business-case-for-curiosity

322 Diane Hamilton. *Innovative Leadership: Developing Curiosity.* Future Learn. https://www.futurelearn.com/courses/developing-curiosity

323 Hal Gregersen & Ed Catmull. *Questions Are the Answer: A Breakthrough Approach to Your Most Vexing Problems at Work and in Life* (Harper Business, 2018).

324 https://weand.me/chad-littlefield/

325 Gary Keller. *The ONE Thing: The Surprisingly Simple Truth About Extraordinary Results* (Bard Press, 2013): 106.

326 Naguib Mahfouz, as quoted in: Amy C. Edmondson. *The Fearless Organization: Creating Psychological Safety in the Workplace for Learning, Innovation, and Growth* (Wiley, 2018).

327 April Rinne. *Flux: 8 Superpowers for Thriving in Constant Change* (Berrett-Koehler Publishers, 2021).

328 See also: Francesca Gino. *The Business Case for Curiosity.* Harvard Business Review. 2018. https://hbr.org/2018/09/the-business-case-for-curiosity

329 Nate Klemp. *Google Encourages Employees to Take Time Off to Be Creative. Here's How You Can Too, Without Sacrificing Outcomes.* Inc.com. https://www.inc.com/nate-klemp/google-encourages-employees-to-take-time-off-to-be-creative-heres-how-you-can-too-without-sacrificing-outcomes.html

330 Kathy Taberner and Kirsten Taberner Siggins. *The Power of Curiosity: How to Have Real Conversations That Create Collaboration, Innovation and Understanding* (Morgan James Publishing, 2015).

331 Rosie Yeo. *Go for Bold: How to Create Powerful Strategy in Uncertain Times* (Major Street Publishing, 2022).

332 Ian Leslie. *Curious: The Desire to Know and Why Your Future Depends on It* (Basic Books, 2015): xix.

333 Paul Ashcroft, Simon Brown & Garrick Jones. *The Curious Advantage* (Laiki Publishing, 2020).

334 Chip Conley. *Wisdom at Work: The Making of a Modern Elder* (Currency, 2018).

335 Dorie Clark. The Long Game: How to Be a Long-Term Thinker in a Short-Term World (Harvard Business Review Press, 2021).

336 Lynne Cazaly. *ish: The Problem with our Pursuit for Perfection and the Life-Changing Practice of Good Enough* (Cazaly Communications, 2019): 31.

337 David Burkus. *You're NOT The Average Of The Five People You Surround Yourself With.* May 2018. https://medium.com/the-mission/youre-not-the-average-of-the-five-people-you-surround-yourself-with-f21b817f6e69

338 See for example: Charles Duhigg. *What Google Learned From Its Quest to Build the Perfect Team*. The New York Times. February 2016. https://www.nytimes.com/2016/02/28/magazine/what-google-learned-from-its-quest-to-build-the-perfect-team.html

339 C.R. Snyder. *Hope Theory: Rainbows in the Mind*. Psychological Inquiry. 2002. Vol. 13(4): 249-275. https://www.jstor.org/stable/1448867

340 Benjamin Hardy. *Be Your Future Self Now: The Science of Intentional Transformation* (Hay House Business, 2022).

341 James Clear. *Atomic Habits: An Easy & Proven Way to Build Good Habits & Break Bad Ones* (Avery, 2018).

342 Oliver Burkeman. *The Antidote: Happiness for People Who Can't Stand Positive Thinking* (Faber & Faber, 2013).

343 Sarah Saravethy's research in: Chip Heath & Dan Heath. *Decisive: How to Make Better Choices in Life and Work* (Random House Canada, 2013).

344 Brené Brown. *Daring Greatly: How the Courage to Be Vulnerable Transforms the Way We Live, Love, Parent, and Lead* (Avery, 2015).

345 Benjamin Hardy. *Be Your Future Self Now: The Science of Intentional Transformation* (Hay House Business, 2022): 47.

346 Jeremy Heimans & Henry Timms. *New Power: How Power Works in Our Hyperconnected World--and How to Make It Work for You* (Random House Canada, 2018).

347 Chip Heath & Dan Heath. *Decisive: How to Make Better Choices in Life and Work* (Random House Canada, 2013).

348 Brené Brown. *Dare to Lead: Brave Work. Tough Conversations. Whole Heart.s* (Random House, 2018): 240.

CPSIA information can be obtained
at www.ICGtesting.com
Printed in the USA
BVHW011500060223
657966BV00020B/681